Blind Spots

Blind Spots

Why Product Development Projects Miss Their Targets

Paul Streit

BEP

BUSINESS EXPERT PRESS

Leader in applied, concise business books

Blind Spots:
Why Product Development Projects Miss Their Targets

Cover design by Cassandra Kronstedt

Interior design by S4Carlisle Publishing Services, Chennai, India

First published in 2025 by
Business Expert Press, LLC
222 East 46th Street, New York, NY 10017
www.businessexpertpress.com

ISBN-13: 978-1-63742-906-8 (paperback)
ISBN-13: 978-1-63742-907-5 (e-book)

Portfolio and Project Management Collection

First edition: 2025

10 9 8 7 6 5 4 3 2 1

EU SAFETY REPRESENTATIVE
Mare Nostrum Group B.V.
Mauritskade 21D
1091 GC Amsterdam
The Netherlands
gpsr@mare-nostrum.co.uk

Description

Product market failures and overruns are pervasive throughout the government and industry, across projects of all sizes and complexities. The statistics don't lie:

- The average market failure rate of a new product is 40 percent.
- The average overrun is 25 to 33 percent or more.
- New technology projects often miss their targets by triple-digit percentages.
- For every 10 percent of schedule growth, costs rise by 12 percent.
- Only three percent of companies complete all their projects.
- Poor project performance wastes 11 percent of investment.
- Only 40 percent of organizations fully realize the benefits of their projects.

By the end of this book, readers will understand:

- Why most new products fail in the market and overrun their targets.
- How hidden incentives drive unjustified optimism in forecasts, budgets, and plans.
- Practical solutions to prevent product market failures and overruns.

And the reader will be able to:

- Develop new products that meet customer needs.
- Hit new product development market, schedule, and cost targets the first time.
- Stay ahead of projects instead of constantly reacting to crises.

There are many books about accelerating product development. However, few address the core challenge facing product developers worldwide. Why do so many new products consistently fail in the market and over-run, often by double-digit and sometimes triple-digit percentages? *Blind Spots* rises to the challenge and tackles this issue head-on.

You can find information on consulting, training, and speeches/presentations, plus free resources to download at https://www .targemetrics.com. The same free resources are also available for download at https://www .businessexpertpress.com/books/blind-spots -why-product-development-projects-miss -their-targets/ or scan the QR code.

Contents

List of Tables and Figures

Tables

Figures

Acknowledgments

Robin Streit—My wife and life partner of 44 years, you are everything! Without your love, support, wisdom, and encouragement, I'd be nothing.

Ryan and Craig Streit—My wonderful sons, thank you for your love and support. I'm so proud of you for your outstanding accomplishments as husbands and professionals.

Mark Sirangelo—Mark, you are the best CEO I have ever worked for and with. You are my mentor and friend. The doors you opened for me changed my life.

Scott Tibbitts—Scotty, thank you so much for suggesting I write this book. I wouldn't have done so if you hadn't encouraged me to take the plunge. Your creativity is the yin to my yang.

Susan Brown—My longtime friend and colleague, you opened the door for me to start my aerospace career. Your advice is always invaluable and wise.

James Voss—Jim, my flying buddy and good friend. We share a love of flying and aerospace. I loved working with you and being your right-seater.

Armen Askijian—Armen, I enjoy our discussions on the challenges of new product development. Thank you so much for your excellent suggestions on improving the manuscript.

Acknowledgments

Foreword

I am truly honored to introduce Paul Streit and this fantastic book to you. I have had the pleasure of working with Paul in various executive management capacities for over 16 years. During our time together, I witnessed firsthand his dedication to the principles in this book and his business philosophy for creative, fast product development, disciplined project management, and profitable business execution. I believe this book is an essential resource for anyone seeking to elevate their operational performance, prevent or resolve new product market failures, and develop the highest quality schedules to avoid overruns.

What sets this book apart is its practical approach to solving the real-life challenges that you face every day. It provides actionable advice about managing the pervasive, consistent problems in product development, emphasizing how to avoid slips and new product failures. In today's rapidly changing markets, it's not enough just to find ways to accelerate product development successfully. As a responsible leader, you must proactively prevent delays and mistakes to ensure your company's new products exceed customer expectations. Paul provides the invaluable lessons you need to stay ahead of your competition.

Having been responsible for programs worth billions of dollars in my career, I was so fortunate to have Paul and his knowledge personally available to help me succeed. He has now taken the wisdom developed over decades of leadership and summarized it for you in this invaluable book. Whether you're just starting in product marketing or project management or are a seasoned product development professional or executive, you'll find that *Blind Spots: Why Product Development Projects Miss Their Targets* offers insights that are relevant, actionable, and immediately useful.

I know you will benefit greatly from Paul and his guidance, just as I did. Enjoy being more successful and staying on schedule!

Mark N. Sirangelo
Entrepreneur in Residence
University of Colorado Boulder
June 2025

Praise for Blind Spots

"Blind Spots: Why Product Development Projects Miss Their Targets *captures what most new products books miss—why brilliant teams still miss their targets. Paul Streit gives a framework to deliver what matters, on time and on budget.*"—**Armen Askijian, CTO, Airbus U.S. Space & Defense, Inc.**

"*Management problems during new product development can result in missing the mark with customers and overrunning cost and schedule. Paul Streit shares his over 30 years of product development experience in this easy-to-follow, practical book to give you the knowledge and tools you need to avoid typical problems and run a successful project.*"—**Jim Voss, Colonel, U.S. Army Ret., NASA Astronaut**

"Blind Spots: Why Product Development Projects Miss Their Targets *is an important, must-read book for any professional involved in project management, product development, product marketing, or product discovery. In a masterful, entertaining narrative, Paul Streit explains how the product development process is transformed by understanding the interdependence of these three disciplines.* Blind Spots *manages a triple play: It's a masterclass in product development, a reference book to keep close when you run into market challenges or overruns, and a transparent, entertaining sharing of the frustrations, triumphs, and lessons learned from over 30 years of personal experience. I challenge you to read the introduction and be able to put the book down. It's that good.*"—**Scott Tibbitts, Founder/CEO Starsys Research Corporation**

Introduction

"I need help with overruns and new product market failures." That's the most common message from my clients and students when discussing product development and project management. AI, computer simulations, modern design tools, and agile development have made designing and building new products easier and faster than ever. However, even though these advancements significantly accelerate new product development, don't expect them to prevent product market failures and overruns. They won't, because the statistics tell the story.

Depending on the industry and the level of innovation, 40 percent of new products fail in the market.[1] The average for nonfood sectors, including chemicals, materials, industrial services, consumer goods, consumer services, investment goods, health care, IT software and services, and technology, is 41 percent. The food sector, which includes baby food, bakery products, cereals, chocolate products, dairy, desserts and ice cream, fruits and vegetables, and ready meals, averages much higher, close to 68 percent. Overruns are higher in the food sector due to multiple variables, including the importance of taste and sensory experience, a complex regulatory and supply chain landscape, shorter product life cycles, increased competition, complexity in understanding and meeting consumer needs, overestimating product potential, and challenges in new product market testing.

It's bad enough that new products fail in the market in double-digit percentages. Schedule and cost overruns are just as bad and sometimes worse. Schedule overruns average 46 percent, and projects deliver

---

[1] Ireneusz Rutkowski, "Success and Failure Rates of New Food and Non-Food Products Introduced on the Market," *Journal of Marketing and Consumer Behaviour in Emerging Markets* 1, no. 14 (2022): 52–61. https://www.researchgate.net/publication/359923834_Success_and_failure_rates_of_new_food_and_non-food_products_introduced_on_the_market.

39 percent less value than planned.[2] Cost overruns average 27 percent. About 17 percent of projects are outliers with much higher average overruns, about 200 percent for cost and 70 percent for schedule.[3]

Regardless of the research study, the performance statistics are consistently within double-digit percentages, with the extremes reaching into triple digits. Market failures and overruns happen irrespective of the company type, industry, team size, technology, product, or service.

There's a common thread here: everyone involved in product development and project management has blind spots that lead them to underestimate their market, schedule, and cost targets with *unjustified optimism*. The book explores several factors that contribute to this cognitive bias, including economic incentives and human nature.

Product marketers and executives working in the front end of product development tend to focus outward, engaging with customers and the industry. They primarily originate from functions such as business development, sales, marketing, and product management. Their compensation and performance targets tend to focus on identifying sales opportunities and growing orders and revenue, which incentivizes them to make aggressive sales forecasts, set low price targets to win business, and demand aggressive development schedules to meet tight market windows.

In contrast, project managers in the middle portion of product development tend to focus inward on project execution, engaging with internal functions like engineering, operations, supply chain management, and finance. Their compensation and performance incentives focus on project schedule, cost, and technical performance targets, which incentivize them to make conservative estimates and forecasts to hit their targets. These divergent perspectives create perverse incentives for unjustified optimism.

Optimistic market, schedule, and cost targets put project managers in a no-win situation. If they push back on the targets, the usual answer

---

[2]Kerstin Balka, Breanna Heslin, and Sina Risse-Tenk, "Unlocking the Potential of Public-Sector IT Projects," *McKinsey.com,* 2022, accessed June 23, 2025, https://www.mckinsey.com/industries/public-sector/our-insights/unlocking-the-potential-of-public-sector-it-projects.

[3]Bent Flyvbjerg, and Alexander Budzier, "Why Your IT Project May Be Riskier Than You Think," *Harvard Business Review*, 2011, accessed June 23, 2025, https://hbr.org/2011/09/why-your-it-project-may-be-riskier-than-you-think.

is, "That's what the market requires, so figure it out." If they say nothing and accept the status quo, they're setting themselves up for failure when overruns inevitably occur in the future. In most cases, they choose the latter for job security, building unrealistic targets into their project plans and assuming someone else will address the overrun risks later.

However, once executive management approves the project plans, they become the official baseline and are often integrated into the company's financial plans and commitments. There's no turning back. Management implicitly assumes the project plan is achievable because everyone agrees to it. This gap in focus between product marketers and project managers is a key factor that drives optimistic market and project assumptions, making it an organizational blind spot that most books on product marketing and project management overlook.

Blind Spots: Why Product Development Projects Miss Their Targets bridges the gap between product development and project management by uncovering the hidden blind spots on both sides—what they are, where to find them, why they matter, and how to address them.

Blind Spots also introduces *Targemetrics*, a discipline I developed over decades that utilizes specially designed metrics and analytical techniques to help you identify and overcome optimistic estimates, enabling you to achieve your product development targets. *Targemetrics* also provides companies, particularly startups with little or no market and operational experience, a foundation of truth to guide product development, make informed strategic and investment decisions, and support problem-solving and corrective actions.

What You Will Learn

This book is different. Instead of focusing on accelerating product development, you'll learn how to recognize blind spots so you can set achievable targets for product development and avoid market failures and delays. You'll become more aware of blind spots at any stage of product development that cause companies to miss key sales opportunities, underestimate execution risks during project management, or miscalculate sales forecasts and campaign resource requirements. You'll also learn why new product market failures, schedule delays, and cost overruns are so common, along with strategies to address them.

Who This Book Is For

Anyone involved in new product development will find this book helpful, as unjustified optimism occurs in all stages of the product development life cycle. If you're experiencing delays, missing development targets, debating about customer preferences, or if your product isn't selling, you're in the right place. This book will help you introduce new products that customers want, on time, and within budget. That's a significant win for you and a source of sustainable competitive advantage.

The book also works well for startups starting from a blank slate, developing new technologies, and introducing derivative products. It also works equally well for agile software development and hardware development. The highly iterative nature of agile software development makes it challenging to make schedule and cost commitments; hence, understanding how unjustified optimism leads to unrealistic forecasts and commitments is compelling.

How the Book Is Organized

Product development is commonly modeled as a life cycle, from initial ideation and concept development through market launch and monitoring, and then repeating the process to update the product as market conditions change. Most life cycles are composed of five to seven stages or more, but a five-stage model will do for this discussion:

1. Ideation and Concept Development
2. Feasibility and Concept Evaluation
3. Design and Development
4. Testing and Validation
5. Market Launch and Monitoring

The book identifies blind spots in product development that lead to new product market failures and overruns and discusses strategies for addressing them. For this purpose, the book consolidates a standard five-stage product development life cycle model down to three stages:

Part I—Target the Right Market consolidates ideation, concept development, feasibility, and concept evaluation into a single stage that encompasses four key topics at the front end of product development. *Start here if your primary problems are with understanding customers' needs, identifying the best sales opportunities, or turning around poor sales.*

- **Chapter 1:** Identify Your Best Sales Opportunities
- **Chapter 2:** Design Your Value Proposition
- **Chapter 3:** Validate Your Value Proposition
- **Chapter 4:** Gain Key Stakeholder Buy-In

Part II—Deliver on Time and Budget consolidates design, development, testing, and validation into a single stage that encompasses five key topics in the middle portion of product development, culminating in the delivery of a new product to the market. *Start here if your primary problems are with overruns or project execution.*

- **Chapter 5:** Overview of Project Management Systems
- **Chapter 6:** Hidden Causes of Project Overruns
- **Chapter 7:** Use Metrics to Stay on Track
- **Chapter 8:** Prevent Overruns with Process Changes
- **Chapter 9:** Manage Resource Capacity

Part III—Drive Sales and Profitability expands upon market launch and performance monitoring to discuss blind spots in creating accurate sales forecasts, planning sales campaigns, and developing bottom-up pricing estimates. *Start here if you're in business development, product marketing, or planning a go-to-market strategy.*

- **Chapter 10:** Plan Order Forecasts and Sales Campaigns
- **Chapter 11:** Drive Profitability After Market Launch

See Figure I.1 for how the common life cycle model and the book's consolidated model relate to each other:

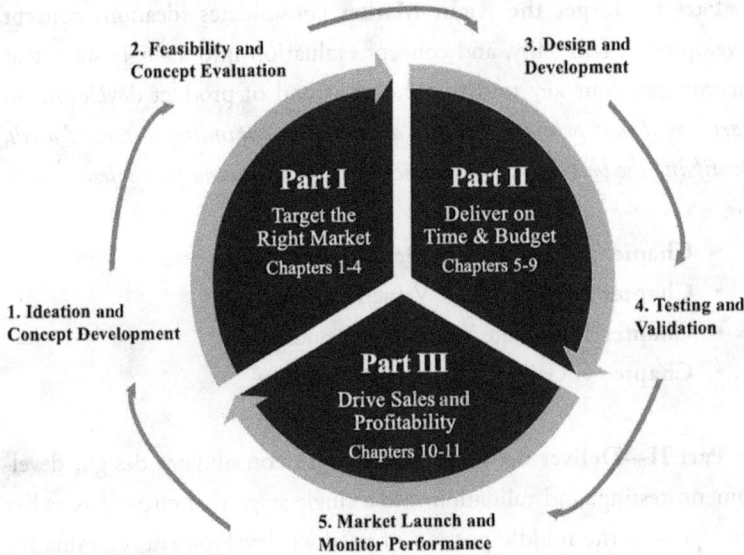

2. Feasibility and
Concept Evaluation

3. Design and
Development

Part I
Target the
Right Market
Chapters 1-4

Part II
Deliver on
Time & Budget
Chapters 5-9

1. Ideation and
Concept Development

4. Testing and
Validation

Part III
Drive Sales and
Profitability
Chapters 10-11

5. Market Launch and
Monitor Performance

Figure I.1 How the book is organized

Each chapter ends with two helpful sections:

- **Reader call-to-action** exercises help you apply what you've learned.
- **Lessons learned** summarize key takeaways in a quick, easy-to-skim format.

The Resources section offers free materials to help you work through the exercises and apply the concepts from the book. You can download the files at no cost under the **Resources** tab at www.targemetrics.com/resources or www.businessexpertpress.com. Consulting, training, and keynote speech/presentation services are available through www.targe-metrics.com.

If only one chapter helps you deliver new products that meet customer needs, on time and within budget, then this book has done its job. Let's get started.

PART I

Target the Right Market

There are many ways to decide which features to include in a new product. However, where many products fail isn't in the design or the technology, though technical issues often take the blame. The real problem is usually not identifying customers' needs and, in turn, failing to ensure the new product or service satisfies those needs.

The book's first part provides a solid framework for systematically and intuitively approaching customer needs and defining products. It all starts with a mindset shift: moving your focus from the product itself to what the customer is trying to achieve while using it.

CHAPTER 1

Identify Your Best Sales Opportunities

Many seemingly valuable new products fail in the market, even with excellent engineering. They fail for a fundamental reason: the product doesn't meet customer needs, despite the company believing otherwise. Misunderstanding customer needs is the most critical blind spot in product development. If your market target is wrong, your new product will fail in the market, wasting all the time, money, and effort invested in its development.

If you ask most people to define a customer need, they'll probably say it's what the customer wants. Well, OK, but what exactly does that mean? Since customers typically have multiple needs, which ones, when satisfied, will motivate customers to buy and offer the best sales opportunities? How do we identify the optimal solution to meet customer needs and test it before starting product development? Once we know the target market, how do we secure funding and approval commitments from executives and other internal stakeholders?

Framing Customer Needs as Desired Results

It's intuitive to think of customer needs as product features or technologies. You see this when companies ask customers to rate their products or services on factors such as quality, performance, or other characteristics. The problem with these questions is that product features and technologies don't correlate well with what customers try to accomplish when using the product or service.

Product features, capabilities, performance, and technologies are all means to an end, not the end itself. What's important is *why* customers want a product capability. Customers are trying to get something done by using the product or service. So, what they care about are the results they expect to achieve or, in other words, their desired results. Defining customer needs in terms of desired results is crucial to everything that follows in this book.

The *desired* part suggests that customers have expectations about what they will achieve by using the product or service. The *results* part refers to how well customers achieve what they are trying to accomplish, which they judge relative to their expectations. Results are variable because their quality may be poor, good, or uncertain. This difference between expectations and reality affects customer satisfaction and, consequently, customers' motivation to buy.

Desired results may be intangible if they are functional or emotional. For example, customers use rideshare services to transport themselves safely and quickly or purchase home workout equipment to become fit and more attractive.

Customers typically expect multiple benefits from using a product or service. Think of what we all achieve every day with smartphones:

- Communications (e-mail, messaging, phone)
- Entertainment (games, movies, podcasts, blogs, social media)
- Education (online courses, how-to websites)
- Search (Google, Bing, Siri)
- Navigation (GPS)
- Internet connectivity (the Web)

Notice that these needs are categorized. They encapsulate many more low-level needs. Smartphone customers have hundreds of needs, organized in a complex hierarchy, although they may not be aware of it. The point is that customer needs are complex and dynamic. You're looking at the wrong target if you focus on the product, technology, or service—because that's the solution, not the problem. It's all about understanding customers' desired results. That's the market target.

It's challenging to shift mindsets from product-centric to results-centric thinking because the former is intuitive and a well-established habit. We all like to start with the solution and work backward to the problem, mainly because we think we know the problem. For example, many years ago, I attended a sales training class. In the first session, the instructor handed me a pencil and asked me to sell it to him. I intuitively responded by asking what features he needed. He promptly replied, "Wrong question!" He then asked another student, and another. Everybody in the class got it wrong.

The right question was to ask what the instructor was trying to achieve with the pencil and why. There are other questions. Why are those outcomes important? Is he satisfied with his current pencil? Notice the emphasis on "What" and "Why." These are different questions from the usual ones about product features, technologies, and capabilities.

Surveying Customers About Their Desired Results

The best way to determine what customers are trying to achieve is to ask them open-ended questions starting with who, what, when, where, how, or why. You don't want a simple yes or no answer. For example, in a men's clothing store, a salesperson might ask—"Why do you need a suit, for work or a special occasion?" "When do you need it?" or "What price range do you have in mind?" Starting with open-ended questions encourages additional dialogue to surface what the customer is trying to achieve and why.

Let's go through an example. Assume our company produces circular saws. It's not hard to figure out that customers use a circular saw to cut wood. That's like table stakes in poker. However, many specific wood-cutting applications exist, like building custom furniture or amateur woodworking. In a real-world product, there may be well over 50 desired results.

Surveying customers to determine their desired results can be time-consuming and labor-intensive. One approach is to survey everyone you know with insights into what customers are trying to achieve and why, then distill the data down to a list, as shown in Table 1.1 (for brevity, the table only displays six desired results).

Notice how the desired results in Table 1.1 are written in active voice with simple language, without referencing any product features or technologies. They're tangible and measurable, relating to customers' expectations. Note that they're also stable: while products, services, and

Table 1.1 Circular saw desired results

ID #	Description
1	Keep the user's body parts out of the cut path.
2	Prevent the blade from going off-track during the cut.
3	Prevent an accidental cut of the power cord.
4	Prevent splintering while cutting.
5	Keep debris out of the user's eyes.
6	Make bevel adjustments easy and fast to implement.

technologies change, desired results don't. Regardless of the type of circular saw the company produces, users must keep their body parts out of the cut path and debris out of their eyes. Products with poor safety features increase the risk of injury, which means customers may not achieve their desired results.

Once you have an initial list, survey customers to validate that it's reasonably accurate and comprehensive. Another way to generate desired results is to observe customers using similar products. What are they trying to accomplish? How well are current solutions performing? You can also combine methods—first compile an internal list and then validate it by asking and observing customers. Once we have a credible list of customers' desired results, the next step is to consider which desired results in the list are most important to customers.

Identifying Customers' Most Important Desired Results

Considering customers' desired results equally significant is tempting, but the reality is more complex. Some desired results hold greater importance for customers than others. We observe this whenever customers make trade-off decisions about which products and services to purchase in a competitive market. They may forgo certain features or capabilities they wanted for a lower price, pay more for additional options, refrain from purchasing altogether, or opt for a different product type. Therefore, it's essential to understand which desired results customers aim to achieve and matter most to them. The only way to determine this is to ask customers directly or observe their behaviors at the point of use.

Rating the Desired Results for Importance and Satisfaction

The first step is establishing a baseline of ratings you believe customers will provide for each desired result. The baseline helps you challenge your assumptions and understand your customers' needs. You can estimate each desired result's importance rating by asking yourself, "How important is this result on a scale of 0 to 10, from 0 = 'Not important' to 10 = 'Critically Important'?"[4]

The next step is to repeat the process with customers. Since you should talk to as many customers as possible to obtain representative perceptions, you'll likely end up with a different Desired Results table than anticipated. These differences are valuable because you'll discover gaps in understanding customers' needs. Use the same rating question you asked yourself and then average across all surveyed customers for each desired result. You may want to plot the ratings to see the distribution. A skewed distribution will distort the average in the direction of the skew, in which case the median will be more accurate because it's not affected by skew.

Customer surveys can be complex and expensive to manage. Most customers are busy, making it challenging to schedule conversations with them. Another option is to survey customers at industry trade shows, conferences, and the like. You must determine where customers spend their time and find ways to meet with them. Some companies use direct mail, contests, and online surveys, or offer a free prize or other incentives to encourage customers to engage in a dialogue. Regardless of the approach, it is essential to understand your customers' desired results and identify which ones are most important to them.

There is one more variable to consider regarding customer needs. Customers rarely start with a blank slate when making purchasing decisions, as they often already use products and services to achieve their desired results. The issue is that they achieve these results with varying degrees of success. Customers won't be motivated to buy anything else if they're satisfied with their current solutions. However, if they're dissatisfied, they'll look for alternative options. As a result, you must also assess customer satisfaction.

---

[4]Anthony W. Ulwick, *What Customers Want: Using Outcome-Driven Innovation to Create Breakthrough Products and Services* (McGraw-Hill, 2005).

To survey satisfaction, use the same methods that you applied for surveying importance. Establish a baseline to test your assumptions and understanding of customers' satisfaction with their desired results, and then survey to gather feedback. You can estimate the satisfaction rating for each desired result by asking yourself, "How satisfied are you with your ability to achieve this result on a 0 to 10 scale, with 0 = 'Not satisfied' to 10 = 'Very satisfied'?"

Compile the desired results, importance, and satisfaction data into a table. See Table 1.2 for our circular saw example:

Table 1.2 Average customer importance and satisfaction ratings
Customer: Amateur home user Product: Circular saw

ID #	Description	Importance rating	Satisfaction rating
1	Keep the user's body parts out of the cut path.	10	7
2	Prevent the blade from going off-track during the cut.	7	6
3	Prevent an accidental cut of the power cord.	8	4
4	Prevent splintering while cutting.	2	4
5	Keep debris out of the user's eyes.	10	3
6	Make bevel adjustments easy and fast to implement.	3	8

Survey data can be voluminous. One product can generate up to 150 desired results; a survey may contact 50 customers. Since two averaged ratings exist for each desired result, there may be up to 15,000 data points (150 desired results × 50 customers × 2 ratings). Analyzing and managing such a large amount of data can be challenging. A good way to reduce the data is to aggregate the desired results into higher-level categories and roll up the ratings accordingly.

In our circular saw example, "Keep the user's body parts out of the cut path" and "Keep debris out of the user's eyes" could be consolidated into a new, higher-level desired result: "Prevent the user from being injured while cutting wood." Similarly, "Prevent going off-track during the cut" and "Prevent splintering while cutting" could be combined into "Prevent cutting errors."

Now that we've identified customers' needs, how do we analyze the data to determine the best sales opportunities that will become the market target for subsequent product development and marketing efforts?

Using the Ratings to Identify the Best Sales Opportunities

We know that customers will buy a product or service if they believe it will help them achieve their desired results. We also know customers won't be motivated to buy unless they are dissatisfied with current results. So, importance and satisfaction combine to determine the sales opportunity for a given desired result. There are four ways they can combine:

High Importance and Low Satisfaction

Desired results with high importance and low satisfaction offer the best sales opportunities, as customers are motivated to purchase. These desired results are customers' top priorities, and they're not getting there with current solutions. You aim to introduce new products and services tailored to these desired results, thereby increasing satisfaction and closing the gap between the importance and satisfaction ratings.

High Importance and High Satisfaction

Desired results with high importance and high satisfaction imply that customers are satisfied with the solutions they're currently using. They will not be motivated to buy because there is no compelling reason to change. A good strategy is to match the competition with similar capabilities unless you can develop a disruptive technology that changes customers' expectations.

Low Importance and High Satisfaction

Desired results with low importance and high satisfaction present a paradox. Customers don't care about these desired results, yet they are satisfied with current solutions. Low importance and high satisfaction ratings seem contradictory because if customers don't care about a particular desired result, why would they be pleased with it? The most likely explanation is that the industry consistently fails to deliver these results to customers, or customers don't believe the industry can improve. Since customers have no competitive alternatives, they reluctantly accept the status quo.

A good strategy is to monitor the market for disruptive innovations or introduce one that improves performance, changing customer expectations. Increased expectations translate into higher importance ratings, which close the gap between importance and satisfaction, motivating customers to make a purchase.

Low Importance and Low Satisfaction

Desired results with low importance and low satisfaction indicate that customers are unlikely to buy, since they don't care about these particular desired results, and nothing on the market has sparked their interest. An effective strategy prioritizes new product development efforts elsewhere and extracts cash for as long as possible.

Consolidating Sales Opportunities Data into a Quad Chart

The easiest way to visualize and evaluate sales opportunities data is with a Sales Opportunities Quad Chart. See Figure 1.1. The chart is a scatter plot, with satisfaction on the horizontal scale and importance on the vertical scale. It's divided into four quadrants corresponding to the importance and satisfaction combinations listed in the previous section.

All ratings for the example's desired results are listed in Table 1.2 and plotted in Figure 1.1. Quadrant I at the top-left corresponds to high importance and low satisfaction; Quadrant II at the top-right—high importance and high satisfaction; Quadrant III at the bottom-left—low importance and low satisfaction; and Quadrant IV—low importance and high satisfaction.

While the example is simple, the quad chart's real power shines in complex markets with sophisticated products like smartphones. The quad chart instantly shows where the best sales opportunities are and what kind of strategy to apply.

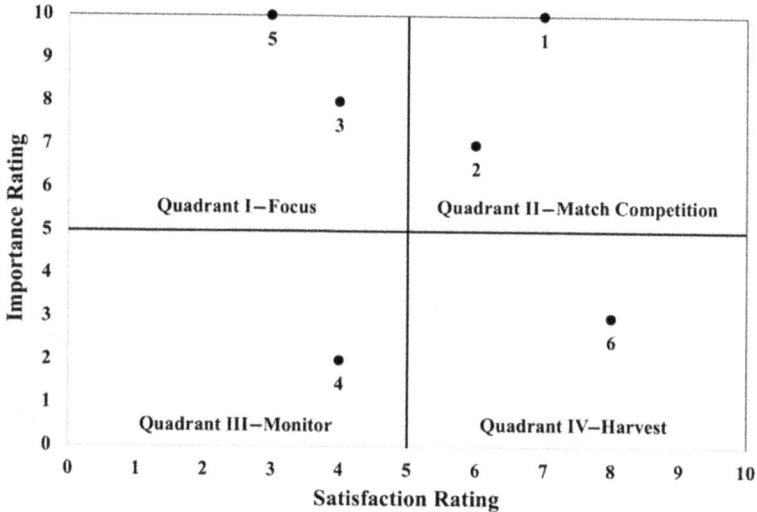

Figure 1.1 Circular saw sales opportunities quad chart

Source: Katz, Gerry. "A Critique of Outcome-Driven Innovation." Applied Marketing Science, Inc. 2008. https://ams-insights.com/article/critique-outcome-driven-innovation/.

I've found that people sometimes think the sales opportunities analysis applies only to blank-slate startups. Not true. The sales opportunities analysis is particularly compelling for derivative products or for understanding why existing products aren't selling well. A key signal that you need this analysis is if you are experiencing internal arguments or debates over what new products to develop, for whom, and for what application. The sales opportunities model even works well for analyzing a Request for Proposal (RFP).

For example, consider a government contractor responding to an RFP for a large system development project such as an imaging satellite, weapon system, or transport vehicle. The RFP typically describes the mission and outlines specifications like reliability, performance, schedule, and cost. It may be tempting to assume that the RFP contains all the information necessary for the contractor to prepare a complete and competitive proposal. However, what about past performance?

Even if past performance is a requirement, will the customer place more importance on incumbent suppliers for risk reduction? How will the customer evaluate poorly performing incumbents versus new entrants with documented good performance elsewhere? What about future product roadmaps? How will the customer evaluate a product compatible with future programs beyond the current RFP versus a product that only meets short-term requirements?

Think of the RFP as a starting point. To win, you must do much more than respond to requirements in the RFP. You must consider why the customer generated those requirements and what the customer is trying to achieve. *You must identify their desired results, associated sales opportunities, and how to respond to the requirements listed in the RFP.* Analyzing an existing product is easier than for something new, but the approach is the same. If you skip the sales opportunities analysis, you're taking a significant risk of missing unstated but essential customer needs.

Assessing Strategy Based on the Best Sales Opportunities

The sales opportunities quad chart helps you assess your strategy by integrating customer input into internal decisions.[5] It also provides a basis for evaluating the product's differentiation. Differentiation changes over time as customer perceptions of importance and satisfaction with desired results change.

As satisfaction increases, so does differentiation and the strength of your strategy. One of the most important benefits of the sales opportunity quad chart is that it forces a strategy to be specific about where to compete. The company may have to develop multiple quad charts, one for each market segment under consideration. Financial analysis can determine which market segments have the best growth and profitability potential.

Another benefit of needs analysis is that it can provide critical insights into customer behaviors beyond what would be available from third-party analyses. Many third-party analyses address only industry

---

[5]Chris Bradley, Martin Hirt, and Sven Smit, "Have You Tested Your Strategy Lately?" *McKinsey Quarterly,* 2011, accessed June 23, 2025, https://www.mckinsey.com/capabilities/strategy-and-corporate-finance/our-insights/have-you-tested-your-strategy-lately.

macro trends. Few companies conduct results-based needs analysis, so the insights gained are a source of competitive advantage. Early detection of market changes can identify how the strategy should change before competitors react.

Markets change often, which means strategy development is uncertain. While results-based customer needs analysis does not give a company a lock on predicting the future, it can provide early warnings of creeping changes if performed frequently enough to keep up with market dynamics. Customers do not necessarily know what solutions they will want in the future because this depends on how well current solutions satisfy their needs. However, customers understand what results they want. Staying engaged with customers makes managing uncertainty easier and less risky.

Customer surveys and analysis based on desired results justify your strategy, which helps gain internal commitment at all levels. If change is required, results-based quad chart data provide compelling evidence and a clear target.

Considering the Risks of Missing the Target Market

Setting the wrong product target can lead to significant product flops in the market. One of the best-known examples occurred in 1985 when Coca-Cola changed the formula of its original soda for the first time in almost a century.[6] Coke was the world's bestselling soft drink, but it felt competitive pressure from rival Pepsi.

Coca-Cola relied on blind taste tests to gauge customer preferences, which seemed to favor a sweeter taste. Many consumers preferred the new version of Coke to the old version and Pepsi-Cola, so Coca-Cola decided to change the formula. However, the company didn't realize until after New Coke's market launch that customers liked a sweeter taste but wanted other desired results. Coca-Cola could have asked additional

---

[6]History.com Editors, "New Coke Debuts, One of the Biggest Product Flops in History," *History.com,* 2025, accessed June 23, 2025, https://www.history.com/this-day-in-history/new-coke-debuts-one-of-the-biggest-product-flops-in-history.

questions, such as, "Do you want your cola to have a consistent and predictable taste?"

Consumers who valued a sweeter taste preferred the new formulation, whereas those who had a sentimental attachment to the brand wanted to maintain the status quo. The company received up to 8,000 calls daily from dissatisfied consumers and some 40,000 complaint letters. One upset customer sent a letter to Coke's CEO addressed to "Chief Dodo, The Coca-Cola Company."

Coca-Cola made a classic mistake. They framed customer needs as a product feature, such as a sweeter taste. The company didn't ask customers why they drink Coke. Of course, the product must taste good, but good doesn't necessarily mean sweeter. To many consumers, good meant familiar, predictable, and consistent. The lesson learned is that we must consider customer needs not as product features but as desired results.

Desired results are not all created equal. Some are more important to customers than others, and customers' satisfaction with current solutions varies for each desired result. We must focus our value proposition on raising customer satisfaction to achieve their most important desired results. High importance and low satisfaction combine to generate the best sales opportunities.

Identifying Your Ideal Customer Profile

You'll want to supplement the desired results and sales opportunities analysis with a concise description of the target customer, also known as the ideal customer. The ideal customer is a hypothetical, perfect customer for your product. The more real-world customers deviate from the ideal customer profile, the less likely they are to be motivated to buy because their needs will change. An ideal customer profile helps allocate sales resources to customers most likely to provide the best sales opportunities.

I worked in direct sales for five years, selling diagnostic cardiac ultrasound equipment to health care providers. I defined my ideal customer as a board-certified cardiologist or cardiac surgeon trained with my employer's ultrasound images in medical school. Their eyes were calibrated to our diagnostic image quality, which helped them improve their patient care. As customers diverged from the profile, they were less likely to buy.

Because I had more sales opportunities than I had time to pursue, I had to prioritize which customers to serve first. The ideal customer profile was an excellent tool to help me determine my priorities.

The ideal customer profile is effective regardless of whether customers are organizations or individuals. In the case of an organization, there may be multiple people who influence the buying decision. There may be one or more user buyer roles that care most about how the product or service performs in the application. Another role may be someone who screens suppliers according to purchasing criteria like price and technical specifications. There may also be an executive role that makes the final purchasing decision and can say no when everyone else says yes, and vice versa. Note that while there may be multiple buyer roles, your ideal customer profile should still focus on the organization. It's OK to discuss the buyer roles, but the organization is still the customer.

In the case of a consumer, the ideal customer profile is about a hypothetical individual who best fits the person most motivated to buy the product. For our circular saw example, the ideal customer might be a professional carpenter who will likely need a high-performance, more expensive saw.

The ideal customer profile should be concise, ideally a paragraph or less. For example, here's an ideal customer profile I wrote from my ultrasound selling days (DEF Company is fictional):

> DEF Company's ideal customer is a board-certified cardiac surgeon or cardiologist who used DEF's cardiac ultrasound equipment in medical school or during residency and fellowship. This customer type knows DEF diagnostic image quality because they trained with it and trusts DEF to provide excellent service, support, and medical education.

Summary

Product development always begins with a clear and concise understanding of customer needs and how they drive the best sales opportunities. These needs become your market target, with which you focus all subsequent marketing and innovation activities.

A customer's need is not some vague want. It's a desired result. The best sales opportunities arise when your product significantly enhances customers' satisfaction with their most important desired results. As this chapter illustrates, there are three key steps to identifying and understanding customer needs:

1. For each market segment you intend to serve, identify the desired results that customers expect.
2. For each desired result, rate its importance to customers and their satisfaction with current solutions.
3. Plot the desired results on a sales opportunities quad chart to identify which desired results generate the best sales opportunities.

Once you have a clear market target, the next step is to design a solution that will increase customers' satisfaction for their most important desired results. This solution is your value proposition, which is the subject of Chapter 2.

Reader Call to Action

A great way to learn these techniques is to apply them to a product or service you're familiar with and use often. The product might be a coffeemaker, office chair, standing desk, water bottle, backpack, or laptop. Professional services might include home lawn care, medical care, dental care, automotive repair, tax advice, wealth management, or legal advice. Think through all the desired results you would want to achieve. Make a list of one desired result per line. Try hard to think of as many as you can.

Remember, desired results are about success *after* customers use the product or service. Write each desired result in an active voice. One desired result for a home coffeemaker might be "Consistently deliver hot coffee with great flavor." Avoid describing product features or technologies. What matters are the results you expect, not the solution that gets you there. Try to list as many as possible, but 10 to 15 is OK for this exercise.

After compiling the list, rate each desired result for importance and satisfaction. Tabulate the data as shown in Table 1.2. Plot a sales opportunity quad chart as shown in Figure 1.1. Desired results in Quadrant

I at the top-left are the best sales opportunities because importance is high and satisfaction is low. Customers will be most motivated to buy if the company can develop a product or service that significantly increases their satisfaction with these desired results.

If you choose a product you love and use a lot, your ratings may fall mainly into Quadrant II at the top-right, where importance and satisfaction are high. Companies will struggle to motivate you to switch based on these desired results, resulting in poor sales opportunities.

Lessons Learned

1. The most critical part of product development, and the most prominent blind spot, is setting the target, meaning identifying which customer needs create the best sales opportunities. If you get this wrong, the product won't sell because it solves the wrong problems.

2. A customer need is a desired result, not a vague want. The word "result" implies the customer is trying to accomplish an achievement, and the word "desired" means the customer's satisfaction with the result is based on the gap between the customer's expectations and what the customer achieved by using the product.

3. Ask customers what results they're trying to achieve. What does success look like?

4. Ask customers to rate each desired result on importance and satisfaction. Avoid asking about product features or technologies. Focus instead on what customers are trying to accomplish with the product.

5. Some desired results are more important to customers than others. Customers are most motivated to buy when specific desired results are important and they're dissatisfied with current solutions.

6. High importance and low satisfaction combine to create the best sales opportunities.

7. Design your value proposition to increase customers' satisfaction with their most important desired results.

8. Focus your marketing and product development efforts on desired results with the best sales opportunities. Address less important desired results as secondary priorities.

CHAPTER 2

Design Your Value Proposition

You've identified your best sales opportunities, so you now have a target and can decide what solution to offer customers. Companies typically consider solutions in terms of product technologies, features, capabilities, and performance. Product-centric thinking is another blind spot when determining the market target. The problem with defining the target strictly in terms of the product is that other factors are part of the solution. These factors include the type of customer and the application. All three factors combined comprise the value proposition. The value proposition will change if any of these three elements change.

Simultaneous changes in products, customers, or applications make the design of value propositions challenging. Many new products fail because companies cannot keep pace with these changes. When they succeed in keeping up, the product often evolves into a complex, one-size-fits-all configuration that strives to please everyone but is complex and challenging to use. Complex products diminish customer satisfaction, creating opportunities for competitors.

The previous chapters described how to set the market target for product development, including identifying customer needs, determining the best sales opportunities, and deciding which product features and functionality enable customers to achieve their most important desired results. This chapter describes how to design a value proposition that satisfies customers.

Defining a Value Proposition

No standard format exists for writing a value proposition. An online search reveals many definitions for the term, some of which are complex.

However, we'll use a simple format with an executive summary, ideal customer profile, target application, customers' desired results, sales opportunities, and a whole product analysis.

Did you notice that product design and technology are not on the list? Morphing the value proposition description into the product or service solution is a common mistake. Leave the design and technology decisions to the development phase since the goal at this stage is to determine what combination of product and application delivers the most value to customers. Notice that the business case and financial analysis are not on the list either, because they have nothing to do with providing value to customers.

A value proposition applies to only one customer type, product, and application combination. Many products implement multiple value propositions if used by more than one customer type or in various applications. It's crucial to document each value proposition your product offers to ensure you fully understand which value propositions represent the best sales opportunities. Each value proposition should be aligned with a sales opportunities quad chart, as discussed in the previous chapter.

We'll review a value proposition example, but first, let's discuss how to identify services and support customers need to use your product successfully. Services and support are critical to your value proposition because your product can't deliver value to customers without them.

Adding Services and Support with the Whole Product

A value proposition won't work unless customers can use it. Think of the product like an onion, where the product is the core, and services and support are the surrounding layers. The combination of the product with services and support comprises the Whole Product.[7]

An airline's core product is transportation from point A to point B. Customers experience additional layers of the whole product when they call the reservation number for assistance, check the airline's app for flight information, or determine their comfort level with the seat and

---

[7] Theodore Levitt, *The Marketing Imagination* (Simon & Schuster, 1983); and Regis McKenna, *The Regis Touch* (Addison-Wesley, 1985).

amenities. These layers of services and support provide opportunities for differentiation and to add value, especially when the core product is a commodity.

Even if a company excels at identifying customer needs and matching a value proposition to those needs, customers may not achieve their desired results if the product is hard to use. The whole product model helps you determine what services and support customers need to use your core product successfully.

Understanding the Layers of the Whole Product

The whole product model is composed of four layers:

1. The innermost layer is called the Generic Product.
2. Moving from the inside out, the next layer is the Expected Product.
3. The third outside layer is the Augmented Product.
4. The fourth and final outside layer is the Potential Product.

Different functions within the company deliver each layer of the whole product. For example, the engineering function typically provides the Generic Product; manufacturing, applications engineering, or field support the Expected Product; project management, sales, or marketing the Augmented Product; and executive management the Potential Product.

The Generic Product

The Generic Product is the core product or service customers buy. You measure it based on product or technology features and trends, new technology requirements, and customer adoption risks.

Table 2.1 provides Generic Product use metrics for the circular saw example from earlier examples. These metrics measure critical product features that execute customers' most important and unserved desired results in Quadrant I of the sales opportunities quad chart. See Figure 1.1. These features are your primary differentiators. You can extend Table 2.1 by adding additional pages for the remaining product features, starting

Table 2.1 Generic product layer

Product: *Professional-grade circular saw*

Feature	Desired result	Use metric and trend	New technology requirements	Customer adoption costs and risks
Power cord guard	#3	10 lbs., 5% weight reduction in 2 years	Need composite packaging	No upgrade or trade-in path
Debris shield	#5	4 settings, doubling to 8 in 3 years	More precise mechanical design	More complex but manageable

with those that satisfy the desired results in Quadrant II of the sales opportunities quad chart. These features must be competitive, but they are not primary differentiators. Product features that deliver the desired results in Quadrants III and IV may be unnecessary because customers don't care about them. However, you should monitor the market because these features could be entry points for disruptive innovations.

The Expected Product

The Expected Product adds technical support, quality, responsiveness, delivery, and cost, abbreviated as TQRDC, to the Generic Product. Services and support may include user guides, 800-number tech support, web chat, online forums, and online tutorials. Continuing the example from the Generic Product, users need to know how to use the new power cord guard and debris shield, including attaching them to the saw during initial assembly.

Most companies need to improve substantially at the Expected Product level. They often treat services and support as cost centers that reduce profitability rather than as an opportunity to differentiate and satisfy customers.

The Expected Product table outlines customer expectations, competitive benchmarks, current supplier performance, and necessary supplier actions to ensure customers can successfully use the product. See Table 2.2.

Table 2.2 Expected product layer

Product: *Professional-grade circular saw*

Service element	Customer expectation	Competitive benchmark	Supplier performance	Supplier action
(T)echnical Support	800 phone, online tutorials, online chat, user guides, community forum	Industry standard	Only online support	Add 800 support within 2 months
(Q)uality	Features work as expected	Features work poorly on competitive products	Features meet customers' expectations	Repeat sales opportunities analysis
(R)esponsiveness	No more than 5 minutes waiting on the phone	20 minutes waiting on the phone	10 minutes	Add phone support staffing
(D)elivery	No retail stockouts	No retail stockouts	At least one stockout monthly	Eliminate retail stockouts within 3 months
(C)ost	No additional costs. Customers expect them	No one offering a power cord guard and debris shield	We offer them	Promote this with safety differentiation

Technical support defines the services that customers expect to use the product effectively. In the example, customers expect help in multiple ways: by phone, online, and through user guides. Because competitors offer these services, they've become industry standards. The company provides only online support, and the product includes a user guide, so the company must quickly add phone support to close the competitive gap.

Quality defines how the product delivers value to customers without errors. The example in Table 2.2 is for functional quality, but it can also be quantitative, such as Defects Parts Per Million (DPPM) or a failure rate in percent.

Responsiveness refers to the speed with which the company addresses and resolves customer inquiries and requests. Table 2.2 illustrates an example of phone support waiting times and callbacks.

Delivery in Table 2.2 refers to product availability in a retail environment, implying no stockouts. When the product needs to be manufactured and shipped, delivery encompasses the entire duration from order receipt to final delivery at the customers' locations.

Cost is the customer's total cost of ownership. The cost in Table 2.2 is described not as a dollar value but as the absence of a price increase. Since the competition doesn't offer critical safety features essential to customers, the company will promote them as safety differentiators.

The Augmented Product

The Augmented Product adds value to the Core and Expected Products by offering customers additional services that replace tasks they currently do themselves, saving them time and money. These services present opportunities to differentiate your value proposition. In the example in Table 2.3, the circular saw company invested in new Computer-Aided Design (CAD) tools to accelerate product development. These tools aren't busy full-time, so the company offered design services to customers to reduce their cycle times.

Table 2.3 Augmented product layer
Product: *Professional-grade circular saw*

Technical task	Cost to customer ($ or Time)	Supplier product/service opportunity	Customer cost deferral value ($ or time)
Computer-Aided Design (CAD)	4 weeks for custom carpentry project designs	We do the design for them to high-level specifications they provide	Saves the customer 2 weeks, a 50% improvement

The Potential Product

The Potential Product is the outside layer of the Whole Product. It leverages new opportunities driven by changes in customers' environments, cost structures, or their customers' environments. Can the company help customers reduce materials or production costs? In the example in Table 2.4, customers' materials costs increased 20 percent over the past year. The company can build parts for customers using its automated manufacturing facilities, which saves customers 15 percent on materials costs due to lower scrap and one week of project cycle time, which reduces labor costs.

The Augmented Product and Potential Product appear similar, but they have different targets. The Augmented Product eliminates tasks that cost customers time and money. The Potential Product identifies customer problems resulting from changes in their environment or cost structure and assists customers in solving them. In the example, customers were dealing with significant material cost increases caused by the outside market and needed to compensate for them. See Table 2.4.

Table 2.4 Potential product layer
Product: *Professional-grade circular saw*

Management function	Customer changes	Supplier product/service opportunity	Customer cost deferral value ($ or time)
Operations Management	Materials costs increased 20% over the past year	We build the parts for customers in our automated manufacturing facilities	Saves customers 15% on materials costs due to less scrap and 1 week of project cycle time

You can't have a Potential Product discussion with customers if you execute poorly on the inner layers of the whole product. Opportunities will open in the outside layers if you accomplish the inside layers.

The key takeaway from the Whole Product discussion is that an ideal product well-matched to customer needs will be successful only if customers can use it. Every layer of the Whole Product must be measured and controlled to ensure the best customer experience. A restaurant with excellent food but terrible service won't keep customers long. Let's tie the preceding discussion together with a simple value proposition example.

Writing a Value Proposition

There are many formats for value propositions, but here's a simple one:

1. Executive Summary
2. Ideal Customer Profile
3. Application

4. Desired Results and Sales Opportunities
5. Whole Product

The basic idea is to summarize your market target and key value proposition for yourself and stakeholders. The executive summary frames the discussion. The ideal customer profile describes the customer. The application describes what the customer uses the product for. The desired results and sales opportunities discussion explains which customer needs the value proposition solves and why. Finally, the Whole Product section discusses services and support that customers need to use the product.

Include the desired results, importance and satisfaction ratings, and sales opportunities data in the appendixes to justify your conclusions in the value proposition summary. An example of a value proposition summary is shown below:

Executive Summary

ABC Company designed a professional-grade circular saw for carpenters who build complex wood products. Professional carpenters greatly value personal safety, given the complexity of their projects and the amount of time they spend using potentially dangerous tools like a circular saw. They expect the product to prevent accidental power cord cuts and provide industry-standard, professional-grade features like multiple bevel settings.

Ideal Customer Profile

The ideal customer for ABC Company's advanced circular saw is a woodworking professional who builds complex, intricate projects like fine furniture.

The Customer's Application

The customer uses the product for professional-grade woodworking, which includes intricate and complex cutting operations. Safety is critical due to the project's complexity, the need for precision and accuracy, and the long-term, extensive use of the product.

Desired Results and Sales Opportunities

The customer's primary concerns are preventing debris from fly-ing into the user's eyes and preventing an accidental cut of the power cord. We will differentiate by providing a debris guard and power cord guide, neither of which our competitors offer. These new features provide the best sales opportunities.

Services and Support

The Whole Product analysis revealed that a lack of 800 phone support and retail stockouts are significant issues for professional woodworking customers. We will provide free 800 phone support to help customers solve their technical problems and increase pro-duction to prevent retail stockouts.

Summary

Your value proposition provides a solution that enables customers to achieve their most important desired results. It's the intersection of a product or service, a customer, and an application. Altering any one of these elements changes the value proposition. Be sure to include services and support in your value proposition so that customers can use your product or service successfully.

Now that you've identified customer needs and the best sales oppor-tunities and designed a value proposition that should meet those needs, your next challenge is to validate your assumptions to ensure your value proposition will satisfy customers. The next chapter discusses how to val-idate your value proposition before committing to product development, which includes writing a Target Customer Scenario and a Positioning Statement.

Reader Call to Action

Write a value proposition for the sales opportunities you analyzed in Chapter 1, Reader Call to Action. See the example at the end of this chapter. Consider how the product delivers your most important desired results and why you buy it instead of competitive solutions. In other words, how does the product raise your satisfaction with achieving those desired results?

Remember to include all the Whole Product layers in the value proposition description. The Expected Product layer is mandatory. The other layers are optional for this exercise, but at least review them to consider how the overall market may change.

If the product delivers multiple value propositions, like a general-purpose product, explain any deficiencies you observe because the product isn't specialized solely to your value proposition. Remember, you are a customer of this product in real life or familiar enough with it to describe its value proposition.

Lessons Learned

1. A value proposition is a proposed product or service solution that enables customers to achieve their desired results.
2. The intersection of three elements defines a value proposition:
   a. Customer
   b. Product
   c. Application
3. If these elements change, customer expectations will change, forcing the value proposition to change.
4. Your value proposition must keep up with changes in customer expectations. Conduct repeat customer surveys as necessary to stay current with market trends and ensure your value proposition remains aligned with customer needs.
5. The Whole Product defines the additional layers of services and support that customers need to use the Generic Product.[8] Companies should not minimize services and support as a cost center, which is self-defeating.
6. The value proposition is distinct from the product's internal design and technology. It's the value that the product offers, helping customers to achieve their desired results.

---

[8]Levitt, *The Marketing Imagination*

CHAPTER 3

Validate Your Value Proposition

Once you've designed your value proposition, how do you know it will deliver the results customers need? Most companies assume their value proposition design is correct without testing their assumptions, which is another blind spot. Not validating your assumptions implies that you will wait until after the product is developed and launched to find out if it works. That's a big and risky bet.

You can validate a value proposition by writing a Target Customer Scenario and a Positioning Statement. The target customer scenario describes how well the value proposition delivers customers' desired results. The positioning statement compares the value proposition to solutions customers already use to help assess differentiation.[9]

Testing Your Value Proposition with a Target Customer Scenario

The target customer scenario describes a day in a customer's life *before* and *after* the product is available. You write a target customer scenario as a narrative. It explains the pain points customers experience while using current solutions and how to resolve them using the company's product. The narrative is emotional, expressing customers' feelings in real time, including frustration, anger, and relief. It also reminds the company who will use the product: real people with real problems.

With a target customer scenario, a company can test its understanding of how a new product will perform when customers use it. Think about the last time a company you worked with messed up. Did it understand

---

[9]Geoffrey A. Moore, *Crossing the Chasm* (Harper Business, 1991).

your problems and what you needed to be successful? Or did it create new headaches for you on top of the ones you already had? The target customer scenario brings customers' experiences to life intuitively and realistically, providing invaluable feedback for product development.

Write the target customer scenario using the following format to ensure your description is comprehensive and the narrative describes the target customer's experiences before and after your product's availability. The template consists of target customer information, a day-in-the-life before situation, interfering factors, economic consequences, a day-in-the-life after situation, enabling factors, and financial rewards.

The Target Customer

This section describes the target customer as a human being. If the target customer is not a consumer, it describes whoever makes the buying decision. The goal is to be as descriptive of the person making the buying decision, including age, gender, economic status, education, and social group role. When more than one person makes the buying decision, they may have different buyer roles. Miller and Heiman describe three types of buyer roles—the user buyer, the technical buyer, and the economic buyer.[10]

The user buyer is the person who uses the product. The technical buyer is the person who can screen your solution based on specs or other technical criteria, but does not use the product directly, like a purchasing agent. The economic buyer is the person who can say no when everyone else says yes or vice versa. In a business transaction, the economic buyer is usually an executive.

For our example, the customer is John, an airline mechanic and maintenance manager on call to fix emergency maintenance issues as they arise. He needs information quickly to troubleshoot and resolve issues. The company sells an electronic, smartphone-based maintenance database system to replace paper-based reference manuals. The header is brief and should only be a few sentences:

---

[10]Robert B. Miller, and Stephen E. Heiman, with Tad Tuleja. *Strategic Selling* (William Morrow, 1985).

John is 45 years old, a Certified Airframe and Powerplant (A&P) mechanic, and the maintenance manager for an operator of corporate jets. He works at JFK Airport in New York and is responsible for resolving mechanical issues with the company's aircraft to ensure flights depart on schedule. The company's customers are wealthy executives who are impatient and demanding, with little tolerance for flight delays.

The Customer's Experiences Before the New Product Is Available

This section describes how users try to achieve their desired results and what happens if the problem continues. The narrative should capture the real-time situation. *What's happening?*

One of the company's jets is stuck on the ramp, unable to depart. John arrives at the aircraft to investigate and resolve why the autopilot-enabled indicator light on the flight deck instrument panel is blinking red even though the aircraft is at the gate and the autopilot is not powered or engaged. The light should be off. Passengers have boarded, and the flight is ready to depart. As John looks at the instrument panel, he realizes this is the first time he has ever worked on an autopilot-enabled indicator light issue. He has no idea what could be causing the problem. John must diagnose and fix the light issue quickly so the aircraft can depart without any schedule delay or upset passengers.

John pulls up the aircraft's maintenance manual and checks the troubleshooting guide. He discovers the guide is missing several vital pages with information he needs to diagnose and fix the problem. John returns to his office to find another copy of the manual. He returns to the aircraft and fixes the light. However, the flight departs more than 90 minutes late. The passengers are upset, and the company must pay the passengers over $100,000 in compensation.

What Went Wrong, How, and Why

This section describes the customer's problem clearly:

> Paper manuals can be easily damaged, vandalized, or misplaced. If field staff fail to notice updates are available or forget to replace obsolete pages with new pages, the manuals can quickly fall out of date.

Cost Impacts

This section explains the cost impacts of the customer failing to accomplish the task productively. For example:

> The light issue delays the flight, upsetting customers and damaging the company's reputation for reliability. The cost impact is $100,000.

The Customer's Experiences After the New Product Is Available

This section replays the same scenario as a day in the customer's life before the product is available, but this time with the new product in place. This section is typically two to four paragraphs. For example:

> John pulls out his tablet and logs into the company's custom maintenance app. The app contains maintenance manuals and repair logs for all aircraft in the company's fleet. John does a keyword search on autopilot-enabled indicator light and finds the relevant information. The documentation is updated automatically in the background whenever updates are released, so John knows he is accessing the latest information.
>
> John searches the maintenance logs and quickly finds the same autopilot-enabled light problem that occurred a month before on a similar aircraft. The database includes an explanation of the root cause, how to fix it, tools required to perform the repair, and a parts list. The app also shows parts inventory, location in the

storage facility, and availability. John submits an emergency parts order through the app, receives the parts, and applies the repair. The flight departs only 15 minutes late. The pilot communicated with the passengers, who understood the slight delay.

The Solution

This section explains how the new product solves a customer's problem:

> Databases can hold essentially unlimited amounts of information, and today's tablets can store data offline. They can be updated electronically in the background when an internet connection is available, and are searchable, eliminating paper-based documentation.

Benefits of the New Product

This section itemizes the costs avoided and benefits gained after the new product is available. Economic rewards are essential for business customers. The target customer scenario must describe economic rewards in tangible and verifiable terms:

> Cost avoidance and customer satisfaction depend on service availability, primarily whether the aircraft flies on schedule. The system pays for itself in avoided losses from a delayed or canceled flight, increased business from satisfied customers, and avoided labor and printing costs related to managing paper updates.

I once bought a desktop PC from a blue-chip brand. I also purchased a service contract to cover any repairs, as PCs were expensive to repair at the time. Cryptic error messages started popping up a few weeks after I bought the computer. After much research, I realized several defective memory circuit boards required replacement. I called the company's tech support number, and that's when the problems started. Even though I purchased a service contract and saved a copy in my files, the company did not have any record of it in their system. I had to scan my paper records and e-mail them to the company to prove what they should have already known. They finally agreed to replace the memory cards, but only after I had wasted a lot of effort and time.

Unfortunately, that wasn't the end of it. The service technicians insisted that I run various software tests that had nothing to do with memory errors. It took hours to run the tests and address the technical issues they caused. After multiple phone calls and more escalation, they finally agreed to send out new memory cards, which, as I expected, fixed the problem. I was so upset that I decided never to do business with that company again. And I didn't. Eventually, the company stopped making PCs, which isn't a surprise given their poor customer service and technical support.

It wouldn't have been difficult for the company to listen to tech support calls to understand their customers' experiences. Their service and support problems were fixable, but they weren't listening or trying to resolve them.

The company's Whole Product had gaps at the Generic Product and Expected Product levels. I was unable to achieve my desired results. Consider your customers in terms of what they experience and what they are trying to accomplish. Write a target customer scenario. You will be way ahead of most of your competition.

Analyzing Differentiation with a Positioning Statement

Once the target customer scenario is complete, the next step is to write a Positioning Statement.[11] The positioning statement describes the target customer, their core needs, the product or service category, the product's key benefits, and how the product is differentiated.

The positioning statement is ideal for 30-second elevator pitches to customers. It is also helpful for explaining to employees and other stakeholders how and why the product will be successful.

---

[11]Moore, *Crossing the Chasm*, 112–14.

Many companies copy their competitors and fail to assess their differentiation. They go straight into product development, which often results in scope creep, a gradual change in product and project requirements. The changes are gradual because they frequently occur one feature at a time. They are also unplanned. As these unplanned changes slowly accumulate, largely unnoticed, they eventually cause surprise overruns. To prevent scope creep, you need a target customer scenario and positioning statement as a baseline to determine how product changes affect the value proposition and differentiation.

The positioning statement includes only two sentences. The format is clear, concise, understandable, and memorable. Many definitions of positioning statements exist in the literature and on the web; some are complex. However, the following format works well:

For [description of the target customer]
    who need(s) [statement of this customer's core need(s)],
    [statement of product category]
    provide(s) [statement of critical benefits].

Unlike [description of the competitive product or service],
    [Your Company] produces [description of the product]
    that [statement of core competitive differentiation].

The following example uses this format. Underlined words come from the template, while all other text is what you would fill in:

For networking equipment Original Equipment Manufacturers (OEM) who need high-speed optoelectronics to link switches, servers, or storage units, ABC Corporation's fiber-optic laser transceivers provide reliable, fast, and cost-effective optoelectronic connections. Unlike traditional wired connections, ABC Corporation produces drop-in, high-speed laser transceivers that reduce delivery cycle times by 25 percent and connectivity costs by 50 percent.

Summary

It's critical to validate your value proposition before committing to start product development. Don't skip this step, as many companies do!

You validate your value proposition by researching and writing a Target Customer Scenario and a Positioning Statement. The target customer scenario describes a target customer's experiences in narrative form before and after your new product or service is available. The idea is to explore from the customer's perspective how the new product or service will solve the customer's problems, in a tangible, intuitive, and verifiable way. The positioning statement condenses your value proposition into a two-sentence elevator statement that describes the target customer, the most important customer needs, the product category, the product's key benefits, and how the product is differentiated.

Once you've validated your value proposition, you have one more step before committing to product development. You must gain commitments from key stakeholders, including executives, board members, investors, partners, suppliers, and others, to secure funding, resources, and support for the product development effort. Gaining key stakeholder buy-in is the subject of Chapter 4.

Reader Call to Action

You identified key sales opportunities in your target market if you completed the Reader Calls to Action for the previous chapters. Your next task is to design a value proposition that delivers the desired results that customers seek. After that, you'll test the value proposition to ensure the product or service will work in the intended application.

Write a target customer scenario for each value proposition you wrote in the Chapter 2 Reader Call to Action. After writing the target customer scenario, write a positioning statement using the standard format. The target customer scenario will facilitate writing the positioning statement, as it serves as a concise summary that combines elements of the value proposition and the target customer scenario. For easy reference, here's the format mentioned earlier:

<u>For</u> [description of the target customer]
   <u>who need(s)</u> [statement of this customer's core need(s)],
   [statement of product category]
   <u>provide(s)</u> [statement of critical benefits].
   <u>Unlike</u> [description of the competitive product or service],
   [Your Company] <u>produces</u> [description of the product]
   <u>that</u> [statement of core competitive differentiation].

Lessons Learned

1. Conducting sales opportunities analysis and designing a value proposition is not enough. You must test how well your value proposition will enable customers to achieve their desired results.

2. Writing a Target Customer Scenario and a Positioning Statement is the best way to test your value proposition before product development begins.

3. A target customer scenario is a written narrative that describes what customers experience before and after your product or service becomes available. The narrative should be intuitive and emotional, capturing a range of emotions, including frustration, anger, confusion, and positive emotions such as satisfaction and pride. The key is to capture the customer's voice.

4. You may discover gaps in your understanding of customers' experiences while using your product. If this happens, you should conduct another customer survey to update your sales opportunities analysis and value proposition design.

5. A positioning statement is an elevator statement meant to be used in real-time customer discussions and to focus your organization on the target customer. It's a written description of the target customer, their core needs, the product or service category, how the target customer benefits from your product, and what differentiates it.

6. Writing the Target Customer Scenario and Positioning Statement may be easier if you first write an ideal customer profile, which describes the hypothetical ideal customer for your product.

CHAPTER 4

Gain Key Stakeholder Buy-In

Funding and staffing to develop a new product are typically a significant commitment. As a result, everyone involved with product development must manage the expectations of key stakeholders, including superiors, subordinates, peers, investors, lenders, board members, partners, and suppliers. Product development can't start without their approval, commitment, or support. The techniques discussed in previous chapters work equally well for key stakeholders because they're still customers, but of a different type. Chapter 4 explains how to apply the same sales opportunity analysis techniques you use for customers to key stakeholders.

Applying Desired Results Thinking to Key Stakeholders

Imagine a scenario where you need the CEO to approve funding to develop a new technology that the company needs to remain competitive. Many people make their case by presenting the merits of the technology. However, starting with the technology is an inside-out view because it begins with the solution instead of the problem. A better approach is to show how the new technology project helps the CEO and company to achieve their desired results. Sound familiar? See Table 4.1.

Reaching key stakeholders, like CEOs, to obtain their desired results and ratings can be challenging. So, you may have to do some research and generate them yourself for a first-pass analysis. Figure 4.1 shows the sales opportunities quad chart for the desired results and ratings from Table 4.1.

Table 4.1 Key stakeholder importance and satisfaction ratings
Product: New technology development project funding decision

ID #	Description	Importance rating	Satisfaction rating
1	Achieve profitability and growth targets.	10	5
2	Ensure the company remains competitive.	9	7
3	Maintain the company's positive brand reputation.	7	7
4	Fund new products with the best economic potential.	5	7
5	Manage business risks to avoid major crises.	9	8

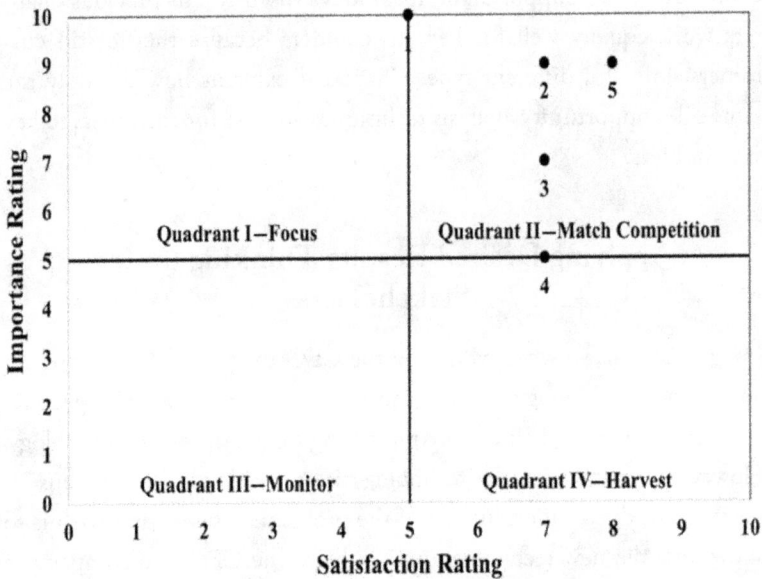

Figure 4.1 Key stakeholder sales opportunities quad chart

Notice in Figure 4.1 that the CEO's desired results cluster in Quadrant II at top-right, which are highly important and have high satisfaction ratings. Because satisfaction with current solutions is high, it will be a tough sell to convince the CEO to approve funding for the new technology project. Go back to your desired results analysis and see if you missed any that would fall into Quadrant I at top-left (high importance and low satisfaction). If so, focus your presentation on how the new technology will help the CEO to achieve these desired results.

To understand how a key stakeholder is another type of customer, I served as a Senior VP partially responsible for investment decisions, including approving funding for new technology development projects. The engineering staff developed an investment pitch that described the technology, how it could be applied, how long the project would take, and how much funding was required. However, the information was incomplete. The team didn't understand that my primary concern was how the new technology would benefit customers and help grow the business. I needed the information they provided, but they didn't consider what I was trying to achieve by funding the project.

I trained them on the material in Chapters 1 through 3, and, later, they made their case that the product would benefit customers and provide growth opportunities for the company. I approved initial funding to start feasibility studies on the new technology.

Introducing potentially unfamiliar terms like "desired results" and "value proposition" might confuse the reader in business justifications. You might want to replace "desired results" with something like "requirements" or "customer needs" and value proposition with "solution." The choice is yours. The key is to think of the material in Chapters 1 through 3 as a mindset that, while designed for use with external customers, is also applicable to help you understand the needs of internal key stakeholders. In the end, the objective is the same: to motivate them to buy, which, for key stakeholders, means deciding on and supporting your request.

Managing Conflicts and Negotiations with Key Stakeholders

Before management funds a new product and approves development, numerous conflicts and negotiations often arise between key stakeholders at all levels. While the primary purpose of the desired results methodology is to identify the best sales opportunities with customers, it can also help manage conflicts and negotiate solutions.

When disputes arise, most people try to resolve them by brainstorming alternate solutions. However, starting with solutions often leads to further conflict because the parties discuss solutions before understanding the problem. More precisely, the parties don't understand each other's desired results. They may think they do, but they don't. As people debate over solutions, they become emotionally committed to the solutions they propose, which hardens their mindsets. Rigid positions inhibit effective problem-solving and exacerbate conflict.

The desired results and value proposition mindsets suggest an alternate way to resolve conflicts. This alternate approach consists of three critical elements: the why, the what, and the how.

The common goal of all parties to the conflict is the why. Without a common goal, the parties would be like ships passing in the night, with no reason to engage in a conflict in the first place.

The what refers to each party's desired results. *These desired results are what success looks like for each party, but not how to achieve them.* Desired results are usually not controversial, appeal to common sense, and are fundamentally reasonable. The only way to know what results each party wants is to ask them.

The how refers to specific solutions that deliver each party's desired results. Solutions are where most conflicts and strong emotions typically occur.

Imagine writing the phrases the why, the what, and the how from left to right on a piece of paper. Most people attempt to solve problems by starting on the right side with the how. Since these discussions focus on solutions, they offer limited opportunity to explore mutual interests, desired results, and the initial reasons for the conversation. A stalemate may occur if differences exist over which solution is the best.

It is far better to solve problems by starting from the left, with the why. Ensure all parties understand their common goal and *why* they are at the table. *There must be a common goal.* From there, move to the right to the what. The parties should ask each other what success looks like and what results they desire or need. The discussion should focus on the desired results, rather than specific solutions for achieving them.

Once the parties reach an agreement and understand what they mutually need to achieve, then and only then, move to the right to the how. Brainstorm solutions that deliver each party's desired results or propose compromises. If emotions become heated or the risk of stalemate increases, move to the left, back to the what, because previous talks may have missed some key desired results. If moving to the what still doesn't work, move to the left again to the why. Remind the parties of the common goal, gain agreement, then move right to the what, gain agreement there, and then move right again to the how.

Remember, move left to build trust, gain commitment, and reduce emotions. Move right only when all parties are ready to resume constructive discussions. Try it the next time you're involved in a conflict, especially in real-time. You'll be surprised by how well it works.

Summary

You need to gain commitment, support, funding, and resources from key stakeholders before kicking off product design and development. Gaining commitment is the very definition of sales; therefore, you must sell the new product concept to key stakeholders. Selling to key stakeholders follows the same approach as selling to external customers. Do you know what their most important desired results are? For example, what is the return on investment? What are the risks? How will the new product be differentiated from the competition? The tools in Part I are equally effective for both internal and external sales. You should use them to provide data as a foundation of truth for essential decisions rather than relying on subjective judgment and opinions that could be biased.

Chapter 4 concludes Part I of the book, which involves setting the correct market targets. The following chapters in Part II address how to deliver on time and on budget. Chapter 5 provides an overview of project management systems as a foundation for subsequent discussions in the following chapters on why development projects often miss their schedule and budget targets.

Reader Call to Action

Recall a situation in your professional life where you wanted a superior to approve a purchase request, hiring requisition, or investment decision, but they denied your request. If you could do it all over again, how would you apply the techniques of Chapters 1 through 3 to obtain a better outcome?

In hindsight, do you feel you didn't understand the superior's desired results before submitting your request? For example, did you want to spend more money than your superior had available? If so, could you have better understood the funding availability before submitting the request? Or was the problem more about your solution, where your value proposition didn't address the key stakeholders' desired results?

Now, reverse the situation. Imagine you were in the role of the decision-maker. Do you think the requester provided appropriate justification for you to approve it? If not, why? As a customer, what did the requester miss regarding the desired results that you needed to approve the request? What was wrong with the requester's value proposition?

Lessons Learned

1. The best sales opportunities arise when customers are seeking their most important desired results and they are dissatisfied with current solutions. The same idea applies to obtaining key stakeholders' commitments, support, and resources.

2. To motivate a key stakeholder to buy, which in this context means to make a business decision or commitment, you can follow the same process described in Chapters 1 through 3. The core idea is to maintain an outside-in mindset to identify what desired results key stakeholders must achieve in return for making commitments.

3. Once you know key stakeholders' most important desired results and their satisfaction with current solutions, you can develop and test your value proposition.

4. Most organizations face conflicts with customers and key stakeholders. By applying the why, what, and how conflict resolution model, organizations can resolve disputes and facilitate effective

negotiations with internal and external customers. The model is easy to remember and applies in real time to prevent escalations and break stalemates.

5. Another way of thinking about the conflict resolution model is to treat any problem as having three components: the why is the common goal of all involved parties (there has to be a common goal; otherwise, there would be no reason to engage in problem-solving), the what determines what success looks like, and the how is the action plan.

PART II

Deliver on Time and Budget

*You've identified your target customer's needs, framed
as desired results, and designed and tested a value proposition.
You also identified the services and support customers need
to use the product successfully. Now that you have a target for
new product development, the next step is to execute the project
and hit your market, schedule, and cost targets.*

*The causes of product market failures, schedule overruns,
and cost overruns are the same worldwide, as they are
rooted in natural human habits and behaviors. This part
brings these causes to light and provides new ideas and tools
to deal with them. If you're responsible for executing new
product development projects, read on.*

CHAPTER 5

Overview of Project Management Systems

Up to this point, we discussed setting the target: identifying the best sales opportunities and designing and testing value propositions that deliver desired results to customers. We've also discussed achieving buy-in from stakeholders. The next step involves planning and executing the development project, which designs and delivers the products and services. Except for simple projects, you will need a scalable project management system to measure and track progress during project execution.

Project management is a well-established discipline with professional organizations, certifications, and university degree programs. Multiple project management systems exist, each with fervent advocates and critics. The most common ones include Earned Value Management System (EVMS), Critical Path Project Management (CPPM), Critical Chain Project Management (CCPM), and Agile Project Management (APM).

Here, we'll cover an overview of these project management systems since most companies use at least one to plan and manage product development projects. Understanding project management systems provides a frame of reference for subsequent discussions on the causes of project overruns and how to mitigate them.

Notwithstanding their value, all project management systems have a blind spot: they inherently assume project managers can thoroughly plan the project and execute successfully against the plan. The statistics say otherwise. As noted in the book's introduction, overruns are consistently within double-digit percentages, with the extremes reaching triple-digit percentages. Market failures and overruns happen regardless of the company type, industry, team size, technology, product, or service.

Blind Spots provides a solution. Project managers must do more than measure progress against the project's baseline plan. They must also measure factors that drive progress on projects to identify and address potential sources of delays *before* the project incurs overruns. It's about staying ahead of the project versus reacting to overruns after the fact. The following chapters cover this in detail.

Earned Value Management System

The EVMS has been around for decades and is popular in heavy construction, government, aerospace, and defense projects. EVMS leverages three key metrics to track progress:

- Planned Value (PV) is the cumulative baseline plan against which to measure progress. PV is the cumulative amount of money intended to be spent monthly over the project's life.
- Earned Value (EV) is the percentage of the PV completed through the current reporting period. EV is work performed.
- Actual Value (AV) is the cumulative actual cost through the current reporting period.

The difference between EV and AV can be confusing. Think of it this way. You can be busy without accomplishing anything. The part that doesn't accomplish anything results in a low EV because only a small portion of the planned work is complete, and the busy part results in a high AV because labor expenses increase.

EVMS can be complex, reactive, and unfocused because it treats all tasks the same, whether they are on slack paths (and therefore can slip to some extent without slipping the project) or on the critical path (where a slip on any task slips the entire project). Specialized software performs the necessary calculations and generates recurring progress reports. Dedicated staff usually feed data into the system monthly and reconcile errors or discrepancies. The software and labor to feed the system are often expensive and complex.

EV measures work completed as a percentage of the plan, meaning that EVMS primarily reflects past performance. This focus on schedule and cost history makes it a lagging, reactive approach. Metrics like

Estimate to Complete (ETC) and Estimate at Completion (EAC) attempt to forecast future performance based on historical data. However, these estimates are often overly optimistic, as delays tend to accumulate and accelerate over time. As a result, past performance is not always a reliable predictor of future outcomes.

Because critical path tasks have no safety margin (slack) to protect against schedule slips, track them separately from slack path tasks. However, since EVMS metrics track all tasks scheduled to start or complete through the current reporting date, it's easy to miss schedule slips in critical path tasks, especially if there's good progress on slack paths.

EVMS adds value by using quantitative metrics and measuring results against the plan. However, it won't prevent overruns because it only measures current progress. In other words, when an overrun is detected, it's too late to prevent it because it has already happened.

Critical Path Project Management

Like EVMS, the CPPM system has been around for a long time. Both systems use a time-phased, resource-loaded task network to calculate the schedule. The key difference is that CPPM is focused on progress directly along the critical path, usually shown graphically in a Gantt chart, but it can also be tabular. Because CPPM reports progress graphically, it is easier to understand and less expensive to manage. Project costs are usually tracked through the company's accounting system and reported separately. CPPM is retrospective, like EVMS, so it will not prevent overruns. However, learning CPPM is less complex and expensive than learning EVMS, so it's more popular, especially in smaller organizations.

Critical Chain Project Management

In the CCPM system, the critical path is called the critical chain. The critical chain is constructed similarly to the critical path, except that it includes a time-only, non-resourced task at the end of the critical path. This task buffers the project's end date from schedule slips. When a slip occurs, the buffer's duration is reduced by the amount of the slip, so the buffer acts like a shock absorber. The buffer task at the end of the critical path is called the Project Buffer. Buffer tasks at the end of all slack paths are called Resource Buffers.[12]

It can be challenging to make room for buffers, especially if the schedule is optimistic. Customers and management often view the buffers as padding and push to remove them. A rational way to justify the use of buffers is to gain agreement with management and customers on the amount of schedule risk on each path and set the length of each path's buffer accordingly. If path-specific overrun risks aren't known, an alternate strategy is to include reserves in the schedule estimates.

Resistance to making room in the schedule for buffers is mainly why the critical chain methodology is not seen as often in practice as EVMS or CPPM. That's too bad because the logic is sound, and changes in project buffer length can be tracked and used as a progress metric. For example, a buffer ratio metric is the ratio of the remaining project buffer duration to the remaining critical path duration, expressed as a percentage. The buffer ratio measures how much of the remaining critical path duration the project buffer protects. If the buffer ratio is 21 percent, then the project buffer can absorb slips of up to 21 percent of the remaining critical path. Any slips beyond 21 percent of the remaining critical path delay the project end date.

Generally, schedule slips of up to a third of the buffer's length are acceptable because some slips occur on most projects. Plan corrective actions to recover or prevent further delays if schedule slips consume 33 to 67 percent of the project buffer. Once slips increase to over 67 percent, take immediate corrective actions because the project's commitment date is at risk. Think of the project buffer as split into three equal zones of schedule risk—color-coded green, yellow, and red. The risk of delaying the project end date increases as the critical path slips further into the project buffer. Again, this metric only works if a project buffer exists in the schedule.

---

[12]Eliyahu M. Goldratt, *Critical Chain* (The North River Press, 1997).

Agile Project Management

The APM system is a project management approach to managing software development that delivers releases incrementally and iteratively throughout the entire product development life cycle. It includes subsets like Scrum, Lean, DSM, and eXtreme Programming (XP). The specifics of these methodologies are beyond the scope of this book. However, APM is addressed here in the context of ensuring that market, schedule, and cost targets are achievable when software development involves rapid and incremental iteration.

The desired results and sales opportunities analysis discussed in Chapter 1 applies to APM because it sets the market target for APM based on what customers are trying to accomplish rather than how the software is supposed to work. The core concept behind APM is to generate small chunks (modules) of software and test its functionality with customers. If the software doesn't work well, developers make changes in the next release. The problem is that the number and timing of new releases may be unpredictable, which makes it challenging to predict schedule and cost performance.

Project managers can significantly reduce the number of iterations if they perform the desired results and sales opportunities analyses *before* APM begins. This way, the releases that implement features and functionality to achieve customers' most important desired results can be prioritized first. Later releases can implement changes to achieve less important desired results. This discussion does not diminish APM. Both methods work and are complementary.

APM is not as common in hardware development because the costs of materials and manufacturing generally make rapid, incremental, and iterative hardware development impractical, at least to the extent typically seen in software development.

Summary

EVMS can be complex and expensive to implement, uses obtuse jargon, and has a learning curve. Its primary benefit is objective, quantitative progress measurements. You'll find EVMS in large construction, aerospace, and defense projects. CCPM is uncommon because buffers can be challenging to implement, and not all project management software systems support it. CPPM is the most popular, and many software tools are available to implement it. APM is well-suited to software development, and it's complementary to the market target identification techniques discussed in Part I of the book.

Don't rely on a task list except for the most trivial projects. Use at least one of the systems discussed in this chapter. If you're in doubt, start with the critical path methodology because it's the foundation for the others. The primary purpose of using a project management system is to measure and track progress, enabling the detection of overruns. Please turn to the next chapter to discover why overruns occur.

Reader Call to Action

In previous reader calls to action, you identified the best sales opportunities, designed a value proposition to satisfy customers' needs, tested it to ensure it works in customers' intended applications, and convinced key stakeholders to support and fund the project.

It's time to plan the project to design and develop the product or service customers will use to achieve their desired results. How would you plan this project? Unless the project is trivial, in which case you can plan and track it with simple task lists, you'll need a critical path task network and project management software to calculate and maintain the schedule.

What project management system will you use? If your project is for the U.S. government or construction, your contract may require using EV metrics. Check out the Earned Value Gold Card online from the Defense Acquisition University (DAU), an agency of the U.S. government.[13] The gold card explains common EV terminology, metrics, and how to chart the data. Most project management software applications compute EV metrics, especially enterprise-level applications.

---

[13]Defense Acquisition University, "Earned Value Management General Reference (Gold Card)," 2024, Accessed June 23, 2025, https://www.dau.edu/tools/earned-value-management-general-reference-gold-card. Some government websites are blocked for international access. Contact the author at info@targemetrics.com for a copy of the source.

Once you decide on a project management system, build a Work Breakdown Structure (WBS) and a critical path task network. Developing a WBS and task network is beyond the scope of this book, but you can find plenty of information online. A great place to start is with free tutorials on Microsoft's website.[14]

Lessons Learned

1. Project management is the mechanism for executing product development. You can find four primary project methodologies:
   a. EV
   b. Critical path
   c. Critical chain
   d. Agile
2. All four methods develop a task network to compute a schedule and track progress, but have different philosophies and metrics.
3. EV can be complex and expensive to implement, and it uses obtuse jargon, so expect a learning curve. You'll find EV in large, costly government contracting, construction, aerospace, and defense projects.
4. Critical path has a passionate consulting community that advocates for it, but it's uncommon.
5. Critical path is the most commonly used, and many software tools are available to implement it.
6. Agile is well-suited to software development, but can be challenging to plan schedules and budgets due to its highly iterative nature.
7. Don't rely on a task list except for the most trivial projects. Use at least one of the systems listed under bullet 1. If in doubt, start with the critical path methodology because it serves as the foundation for the others.

---

[14]Microsoft, "Create a Project in Project Desktop," *Microsoft Support*, n.d., accessed June 23, 2025, https://support.microsoft.com/en-us/office/create-a -project-in-project-desktop-783c8570-0111-4142-af80-989aabfe29af.

CHAPTER 6

Hidden Causes of Project Overruns

Although many leaders invest significant time and effort in carefully planning product development projects, the statistics show that they often encounter market failures, schedule delays, and budget overruns. These challenges lead to missed market opportunities, dissatisfied customers, diminished brand value, and financial losses. This section will investigate the causes of overruns, followed by subsequent chapters that introduce new ideas and tools to prevent or alleviate them.

Major David D. Christiansen of the U.S. Air Force published an informative study of 64 overrun Department of Defense (DOD) projects. The study documented the widespread nature of cost and schedule optimism in development projects. Christiansen compared actual cost overruns at different stages of project completion to projected final cost overruns.

The comparison revealed that projected overruns were excessively optimistic throughout each project's lifespan. The contractors were at least 50 percent optimistic, while the government was 25 percent optimistic. Although the government's estimates were more accurate than those of the contractors, both remained wildly optimistic and far from actual performance. The results proved insensitive to contract type, contract phase, product type, and military branch.

The data revealed that when projects overrun after reaching at least 10 percent completion, they never catch up. Consequently, overruns accumulate over time. The growth rate of overruns stabilizes between 30 percent and 50 percent completion as the project transitions from initial design to assembly, integration, and testing. For every 10 percent increase in schedule growth, costs rise by an average of 12 percent.

Although Christiansen published his study in 2015, the percentages remain essentially unchanged over time because the causes of overruns are systemic and rooted in human behavior. These behaviors are blind spots, embedded in an organization's policies, procedures, and culture.

Since you can't change behaviors you can't see, overruns are a persistent problem for everyone. Root causes for overruns include:

- Failing to recognize and manage uncertainty.
- Using aggressive targets to avoid overruns.
- Tracking projects using only lagging indicators.
- Failing to manage resource overloads.
- Funding projects without reserves to protect against overruns.
- Underestimating due to the planning fallacy.
- Adopting a get-it-sold-and-keep-it-sold-mindset.
- Assessing risks optimistically.
- Underinvesting in technical execution.
- Exhibiting unjustified optimism.

Failing to Recognize and Manage Uncertainty

Most significant overruns occur where uncertainties are highest, particularly in technology development. Technology development is risky because it requires innovation, which involves learning. Learning involves making mistakes and repeating work. As a result, innovation makes technology development inherently unpredictable. Because derivative products involve less innovation, they're less risky.

Aside from innovation, uncertainty causes delays due to the combination of random variation and sequential operations.[15] Random variation can lead to some tasks taking longer than planned. Since tasks are often sequential, delays accumulate because upstream tasks are the starting point for downstream activities. Downstream activities typically lack reserves to recover from delays, resulting in project slippage. These delays may appear as poor execution by the project team, but the underlying cause is simply random variation combined with sequential operations.

---

[15]Goldratt, *Critical Chain.*

Using Aggressive Targets to Avoid Overruns

Another common cause of overruns is setting aggressive targets, with the expectation that projects will overrun anyway, so why not set aggressive targets and receive the product earlier? The problem with this thinking is that aggressive targets are more likely to exacerbate overruns because they are, by definition, optimistic.

For example, customers and executives are aware that most suppliers and development projects will miss their targets. As a result, they compensate by demanding more aggressive delivery schedules than they need, with the logic that the additional schedule margin will absorb any slips. While this thinking is logical, it's also misguided.

Vendors and project teams will struggle to meet the more aggressive delivery schedules. The projects will inevitably overrun, reinforcing customer expectations and encouraging even more aggressive future targets, creating a race to the bottom where everyone loses.

Tracking Projects Using Only Lagging Indicators

There are two key metrics for tracking performance: leading and lagging indicators. Neither is inherently good nor bad; both are essential for measuring and monitoring progress.[16]

Leading metrics evaluate the progress of operational activities that drive strategic outcomes. These activities typically occur at lower organizational levels, making them invisible to executives, who often focus on high-level strategic metrics such as revenue and profitability. However, strategic metrics are lagging indicators, meaning they reflect events that have already occurred. Depending on only lagging indicators is acceptable if you want to understand what happened, but it's problematic if your goal is to prevent an unfavorable outcome. Schedule and cost performance metrics are also lagging indicators, as they only disclose overruns after they have taken place. The objective should be to anticipate overruns before they happen.

In most organizations, people often operate reactively without realizing it. Executives primarily monitor lagging financial performance

---

[16]Chris McChesney, Sean Covey, and Jim Huling. *The 4 Disciplines of Execution: Achieving Your Wildly Important Goals* (Free Press, 2012).

metrics. Project teams and mid-level managers track their projects using lagging schedule and cost metrics. No one uses leading metrics to assess progress on key activities that drive strategic performance, preventing organizations from anticipating and addressing problems *before* they escalate into overruns.

For instance, if a company wins a new contract that requires hiring additional engineering staff, the contract's schedule and cost baseline plans will include time and cost estimates to hire the extra engineers. However, if recruiting new engineers takes longer than anticipated, there will be fewer engineers available to design the product, which may result in the project falling behind schedule. Therefore, the engineering hiring rate acts as a leading indicator of project success.

A useful metric for measuring the engineering hiring rate is to track cumulative daily hiring against cumulative daily planned hiring. When cumulative daily hiring lags behind planned hiring, the project may fall behind schedule, requiring management to add more recruiters to recover and prevent an overrun.

Every strategic goal should have a corresponding lagging metric to measure progress and at least one leading metric to evaluate the performance of critical activities that drive progress toward the strategic goal. Without leading metrics, you're setting yourself up for surprises and bad outcomes because you don't know what drives project success or how well those activities are performing.

Failing to Manage Resource Overloads

Companies struggle to align resource capacity with demand, which leads to resource overloads due to multitasking and unregulated workflows. Managers feel pressured to meet service demands, causing them to spread their resources across too many projects. Although multitasking appears productive, it exacerbates resource overloads and delays.[17] See Figure 6.1.

---

[17]Daniel Kahneman, and Amos Tversky, "Intuitive Prediction: Biases and Corrective Procedures," *Defense Technical Information Center*, 1977, accessed June 23, 2025, https://apps.dtic.mil/sti/tr/pdf/ADA047747.pdf. Some government websites are blocked for international access. Contact the author at info@ targemetrics.com for a copy of the source.

(1)	Tasks	1		2		3	

⊢ —— 10 —— ‖—— 10 ——‖— 10 ——⊣

(2)	Subtasks	1a	1b	2a	2b	3a	3b

⊢ 5 ‖ 5 ‖ 5 ‖ 5 ‖ 5 ‖ 5 ⊣

(3) Multi-tasking	1a	2a	3a	1b	2b	3b

⊢ 5 ‖ 5 ‖ 5 ‖ 5 ‖ 5 ‖ 5 ⊣

(4)	Task 1	1a	2a	3a	1b	Task 1 Complete

⊢ 5 ‖ 5 ‖ 5 ‖ 5 ⊣

Each task is completed after 20 days, but 10 of those days were spent on other tasks.

(5)	Task 2	2a	3a	1b	2b	Task 2 Complete

⊢ 5 ‖ 5 ‖ 5 ‖ 5 ⊣

(6)	Task 3	3a	1b	2b	3b	Task 3 Complete

⊢ 5 ‖ 5 ‖ 5 ‖ 5 ⊣

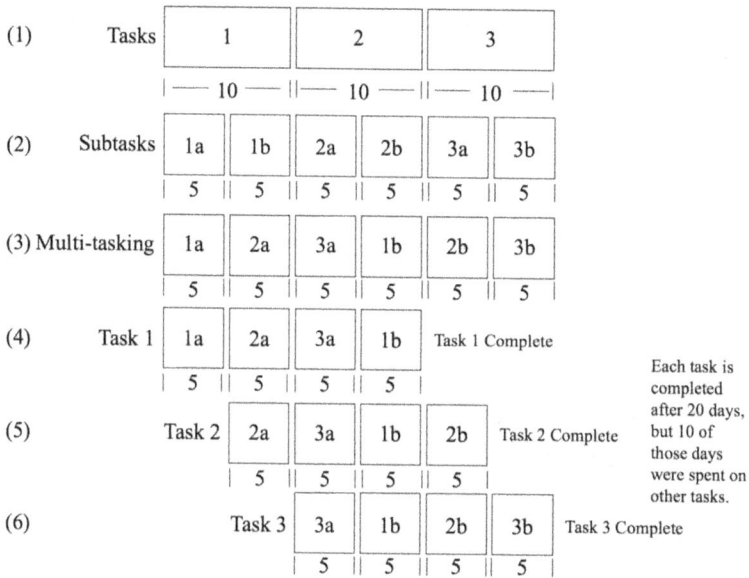

Figure 6.1 Multitasking impacts

Line 1 in Figure 6.1 shows a simple project with three sequential tasks. Each task lasts 10 days, so the project lasts 30 days. Assume one resource is available. Line 2 splits each task into two subtasks, each lasting five days, which is 50 percent multitasking.

Line 3 illustrates the sequence of subtasks the resource executes to complete the project. The resource engages in all main tasks simultaneously through multitasking. The resource begins and finishes Subtask 1a, then shifts to Subtask 2a, and subsequently moves to Subtask 3a. All three tasks have commenced and are underway, but only the first half of each task is complete. The resource then completes Subtask 1b (the second half of Task 1), switches to Subtask 2b, and finally to Subtask 3b. Once Subtask 3b is complete, the project is complete.

Lines 4, 5, and 6 illustrate the subtask sequences for Tasks 1, 2, and 3, respectively. Task 1 completes once Subtasks 1a and 1b are complete. Subtask 1b is postponed for 10 days while the resource focuses on Subtasks 2a and 3a. Each task takes 20 days to process, consisting of 10 days of work followed by a 10-day delay while the resource is busy elsewhere.

The tasks overlap on paper, which compensates for delays caused by subtasks awaiting resources. As a result, the project seems poised to finish in 30 days as planned. However, *this is an illusion* because multitasking leads to further delays from repeated setups and teardowns, catching up on previous tasks, and troubleshooting errors caused by frequent switching. Moreover, the 10-day wait for each task while the resource works elsewhere increases the likelihood of unplanned interruptions, equipment failures, priority shifts, and requirement changes that further delay the project.

The example in Figure 6.1 only shows multitasking *within* a project. In most organizations, multitasking also occurs *across* projects. Multitasking across projects is far more dynamic, complex, and disruptive than within projects because multiple projects are delayed instead of only tasks. The net result is that the entire project portfolio is subject to escalating schedule overruns. The solution is to regulate workflow through critical resources, which the book covers in detail in Chapter 9, Manage Resource Capacity.

Funding Projects Without Reserves to Protect Against Overruns

Executive management and customers are rarely willing to fund reserves to protect against overruns. Executives perceive reserves as a form of sandbagging, allowing project teams to achieve their performance targets more easily. Customers perceive reserves as the supplier's attempt to increase profitability without adding value. They also question why they should pay more to fund a supplier's potentially poor performance.

Even when estimators include reserves, competition often bargains them away. All it takes is for one competitor to bid aggressively. Other competitors respond by cutting their prices to remain competitive. Price reductions reduce profitability, which forces unplanned cost cuts. Reserves are often the first to go. Once projects fall behind, they can't catch up without reserves to absorb the overruns. Overruns will continue to accumulate until the project is complete.

This discussion assumes reserves protect the project's end date from delays. An alternative option is to begin the project earlier by the reserve amount, ensuring delays won't affect the required completion date. However, using reserves or starting earlier won't be effective if the project duration exceeds the time from today to the required date or if starting early isn't feasible. Additionally, you may encounter structural obstacles to starting earlier, such as waiting for the customer's RFP. Nevertheless, cost overruns are so common that using reserves as a hedge is prudent.

I worked in the desktop PC hard disk drive industry for five years. The development cycle for a new generation of desktop PC disk drives typically took 18 months to two years, including overruns, depending on whether the new generation was a derivative product or a new technology. However, the market window was shorter, six months to a year. If companies initiated development within a year of the market window, they faced a high risk of missing it. The only solution was to start at least two years before the market window. Early starts were standard because missing the window could put a company out of business.

Underestimating due to the Planning Fallacy

The Planning Fallacy is a human cognitive bias where people underestimate the time, costs, and resources required to complete future tasks and projects, even when their past experiences or the experiences of others suggest otherwise. This bias often leads to unjustified optimism, a blind spot in price and schedule estimates. This same bias also leads people to overestimate the benefits of future tasks, such as the amount and timing of future revenue.[18]

Think back to the last time you did something that you had never done before. For example, you might have assembled a child's toy or designed and built a custom piece of furniture. Before you started working on the project, what were your expectations for how long it would last? You likely exceeded your initial estimates by a significant margin. That's

---

[18]Kahneman and Tversky, "Intuitive Prediction".

the planning fallacy in action. Experience is the best cure to offset inherent optimism. If you don't have relevant experience, then look to the experience of others, especially on projects of similar size and complexity.

Adopting a Get-It-Sold-and-Keep-It-Sold Mindset

Companies have many incentives to pursue orders aggressively. These incentives include competition, growth targets, sales forecasts, performance bonuses, and job security. As previously discussed, bids and cost estimates are often naturally optimistic, setting the stage for future overruns and losses. It may take years before overruns become apparent, causing management to overlook the get-it-sold actions and blame the project team. Recognizing get-it-sold actions is essential before the company commits to delivery schedules and pricing. The following two chapters discuss how to identify this process.

Strong incentives exist to continue a project or contract even after its economic justification has ceased to exist. Incentives to keep it sold may include contractual obligations, dedication to the mission, avoiding job cuts, spending the allocated budget, political ramifications (especially in the government), or avoiding reputational harm. Keeping it sold is the other half of getting it sold. Both contribute to long-term overruns and are challenging to overcome.

The following chapters discuss innovative solutions for unjustified, pervasive optimism in schedule and cost estimates.

Assessing Risks Optimistically

Traditional risk management is limited to what is foreseeable, even though unknown and unknowable risks exist. How should unknown and unknowable risks be managed? The most common solution is to treat them as a class in the project's risk register without trying to be specific. Companies sometimes include allocations in the risk register for unknown and unknowable risks. This allocation is typically minor because there's no information to justify a higher allocation.

If you think about it, allocating a small budget makes no sense. Overruns, by their nature, are the result of unplanned activities. Since these activities were unplanned, the project team did not expect them to occur, which suggests they were unknown or unknowable (at least to that project team at that time).

The best way to account for unknown and unknowable risks is to use Reference Class Forecasting (RCF) to review actual schedule and cost performance for projects of equivalent complexity and size, whether internal or external to the company. For example, suppose known risks in the risk register could result in a 15 percent overrun, but other projects of similar size and complexity generate 25 percent overruns. In that case, adding at least 10 percent to the risk register makes sense. If the causes of overruns in other projects are known, add the additional risks to the risk register; otherwise, classify them as unknown and unknowable.

Most organizations apply well-known risk management techniques to identify and mitigate risks.[19] The conventional approach is to identify risks, estimate their probabilities of occurrence and impacts, and then define a mitigation plan to prevent them from occurring. Risk analysis can be qualitative or quantitative.

Quantitative risk analysis uses statistical analysis to estimate a risk's impact, which helps prioritize resource allocation for mitigation. Each risk has an expected value equal to the probability of the risk times the cost impact. For example, if the likelihood of a test failure is 25 percent and the cost impact of corrective actions is $100,000, the risk's expected value is $25,000. Expected values are well-suited for items produced and consumed in high volumes, such as consumer products. The high volume provides a large amount of data, making expected value probability calculations more accurate. Expected values are inaccurate for complex, custom products produced in low volumes, such as those for space missions.

Qualitative risk analysis generally involves a subjective rating system to assess risks. It is particularly effective for risks that are difficult to quantify or measure, such as geopolitical, macroeconomic, or emerging

---

[19]Rachel Rotich, "Risk Analysis in Project Management: Steps and Benefits," *Indeed.com*, 2022, accessed June 23, 2025, https://www.indeed.com /career-advice/career-development/risk-analysis-project-management.

technology risks. These risks are unpredictable due to the lack of objective past performance data to inform probability and cost impact assessments.

The qualitative risk rating system comprises a subjective rating table that assigns risk ratings based on the probability of occurrence and the impact of each risk. The list includes a description, probability, impact rating, and risk score for each risk. Sorting the risks in descending order by the risk score places the highest risks at the top of the list, helping to ensure they are the top priority for mitigation efforts. Refer to Table 6.1 for the rating definitions and Table 6.2 for the risk list for the circular saw examples from previous chapters.

Table 6.1 Qualitative risk analysis subjective ratings

Impact	Probability of occurrence		
	1 = Low	2 = Medium	3 = High
3 = High	3	6	9
2 = Medium	2	4	6
1 = Low	1	2	3

Table 6.2 Circular saw technology risks list

Risk Description	Likelihood rating	Impact rating	Risk score
The debris shield shatters upon impact.	2	3	6
Splintering occurs due to a dull blade.	2	2	4
Power cord guard fasteners fail.	1	2	2

The columns in Table 6.1 represent ratings of the probability of occurrence of a risk. The rows represent ratings of impacts if the risk materializes. A risk's calculated risk score is the product of its probability rating times its impact rating. For example, if a risk's probability rating is medium and its impact rating is high, the risk score is $2 \times 3 = 6$.

The risk estimating team compiles the list as shown in Table 6.2 through research and brainstorming to identify all foreseeable project risks. The project team would first focus on mitigating the debris shield's shattering upon impact, which has the highest risk score. They can address the other risks once resources become available.

Regardless of the method, risk management methodologies should be rigorous, systematic, and comprehensive. However, product failures and unplanned project overruns still occur because risk estimation has blind spots, particularly with risks lurking in the background of organizational systems, policies, and procedures. Project teams often overlook these risks, which leads to their exclusion from risk analyses. For instance, few project teams recognize multitasking as a risk despite its high probability and impact.

Project teams often accept low-probability, low-impact risks as inconsequential. The problem is that a chain of low-probability, low-impact events can combine to create high-impact events. Airline accidents are like this: a chain of events, each low-risk and low-impact, combine to cause a tragedy. Preventing the accident involves breaking at least one of the links in the chain by preventing that risk from occurring. Risk chains rarely factor into project risk analysis because they are hard to identify and predict. Most risk models consider risks in isolation.

Complex, systems-level risks are difficult to estimate and mitigate, especially for aerospace and defense projects that involve developing some of the world's most complex and technically challenging products. Because of complex interfaces and data flows between subsystems, systems-level risks can be difficult to predict and assess. Complex risks are often treated as unknown and unknowable until failures occur, after which teams know where to look.

Project risk analysis is far from exhaustive. However, risk analysis is still valuable for identifying, assessing, and mitigating risks that the project team can identify. It's crucial to recognize that many risk analyses overlook organizational and system-related risks, a significant reason why market failures and overruns persist.

Underinvesting in Technical Execution

Technical issues in new product development are often specific to the technology and type of product. However, in my over 30 years of experience in four high-tech businesses, common themes emerged regarding technical mistakes:

- Designing the product before understanding customer needs.
- Inadequate testing, especially in the customer's application.
- Poor design for manufacturability and testability.
- Deficient systems engineering.
- Poor design configuration and revision control.
- Poor tolerance analysis and control.
- Inadequate regulatory compliance in regulated businesses.
- Ignoring that innovation requires learning, risking overruns.
- Multitasking critical technical resources across product development projects.
- Inadequate design standards, design tools, and technical training.
- Poorly written procedures.
- A lack of discipline in following procedures.

Innovation by necessity involves learning and making mistakes. That's OK. However, the issues listed are not part of innovation; they're part of the management system and can have severe consequences. Here are some real-world examples.

In September 2003, a satellite manufacturing team at a government contractor's facility intentionally tilted a satellite from a vertical orientation to horizontal as part of standard manufacturing operations.[20] As the satellite tipped, it slipped from its mounting mechanism and fell to the floor. Fortunately, no one was injured, but the accident nearly destroyed the satellite.

A formal investigation determined that the contractor failed to follow procedures to properly configure the mechanical mounting platform before placing and tilting the satellite. The contractor's operations team did not install 24 bolts to secure the satellite. Instead, they relied on documentation without visual and mechanical verification, as required by the procedures.

---

[20] Jeff Foust (SpaceRef), "NOAA-N-Prime Satellite Mishap Investigation Report Released," SpaceNews, 2004, accessed June 23, 2025, https://spacenews.com/noaa-n-prime-satellite-mishap-investigation-report-released/.

The investigation also found the entire operation had systemic issues. The manufacturing team was inadequately staffed, complacent, and rushed. They also planned their operations poorly. They disregarded safety procedures and failed to notify safety representatives about the operation. Red lines (edits) to the procedures were poorly implemented and controlled, and the process documentation was vague. The team did not follow procedures and waived process steps due to the inadequate participation of quality assurance staff from both the contractor and the government. The most significant problem was that all parties treated flight hardware as a routine operation rather than prioritizing mission, product, and personnel safety.

The contractor had to rebuild at least 15 percent of the satellite. The contractor forgave all profits from the contract and also wrote off a $30 million charge against earnings. The U.S. government covered the remaining $135 million in repair costs. The mishap delayed the project schedule for a few years, but eventually, they launched the satellite, which operates today.

As an aerospace and defense contractor executive, I encountered similar situations, one almost comical if the overruns weren't so severe. We were manufacturing a constellation of small communications satellites for a commercial customer. A large aerospace company designed and built the payload (the part of the satellite that performs the mission). The payload transmitted and received signals with ground stations through the primary antenna, which pointed toward the Earth while in orbit.

The payload manufacturer unintentionally reversed the design of the connection interface between the antenna and the payload, causing signals to transmit through the bottom of the antenna instead of the top. Reversing the antenna's polarity caused the signals to beam into space instead of to ground stations on the Earth. Even worse, the signal energy passed through the spacecraft before heading out to space. The generated signal energy interfered with the spacecraft electronics, causing various technical problems.

One would think that prototype testing of the communications system would discover a connection reversal. Still, through bad luck, the test engineers accidentally reversed the antenna test fixture, which corrected the prototype's antenna connection reversal. Sequential reversals resulted in regular satellite operation.

Because prototype testing proved the satellite design was functional, the customer decided not to test the antenna function in production. There was still an opportunity to discover the design flaw during ground noise testing of the entire satellite. Engineers noticed a large amount of electronic noise in the spacecraft generated by the reversed antenna, but they falsely diagnosed the problem as poor noise shielding in the spacecraft's electronics. They added shielding until the noise stopped, making the spacecraft ready for flight.

After the launch, we quickly discovered the mistake because the ground stations received weak spacecraft transmissions. The engineers eventually solved the problem by flipping the satellites upside down to point the antenna *away* from the Earth, which allowed the reversed signals to reach the ground stations. However, flipping the satellites caused other technical issues that the team eventually resolved, but only after extensive overruns and considerable embarrassment.

Exhibiting Unjustified Optimism

If there's one comprehensive theme about overruns and product market failures, it's unjustified optimism. *Overruns are relative to performance expectations.* A project may take longer or cost more than expected, but is this due to unrealistic expectations or execution issues? The common assumption is poor execution, but if the schedule and budget don't accommodate the level of innovation required, overruns will occur even if the project team executes flawlessly. Management falsely assumes the baseline is realistic when, in fact, it's optimistic.

There may be legitimate strategic reasons to plan and bid aggressively. That's OK, provided stakeholders expect and prepare for future overruns. After a contract win, everyone except the project team tends to forget that the plan was aggressive. A hidden assumption is that the project will execute on schedule and within budget, which it can't. Eventually, the project will overrun, especially during prototype builds.

NASA's Commercial Crew program is an excellent example of how overruns work. In 2014, NASA awarded contracts to Boeing and SpaceX to develop human-rated spacecraft to transport astronauts to and from the International Space Station (ISS). NASA expected both contractors to achieve flight certification by 2017, a three-year development cycle. Boeing's contract award was $4.2 billion. SpaceX's was $2.6 billion.[21]

SpaceX achieved NASA flight certification in November 2020, three years late against a three-year baseline schedule, a 100 percent schedule overrun. SpaceX is privately held and does not announce cost overruns. As of mid-2025, Boeing has not yet achieved NASA flight certification. Since the project started in 2014, the actual total duration has been about 11 years. The project was supposed to take three years, so the schedule overrun is eight years or 267 percent. As of early February 2025, Boeing's cumulative overrun on its Starliner Commercial Program is over $2 billion, or about 48 percent.[22]

Developing human-rated spacecraft is one of the most challenging projects in aerospace and defense, requiring extensive innovation to overcome extreme technical risks. However, neither company was the first to develop a human-rated spacecraft, so why did they experience such severe overruns?

The Commercial Crew program was the first human-rated spacecraft development project for both contractors. Boeing had experience developing the human-rated Apollo program command and service module, but that was in the 1960s with a different, long-retired project team. Boeing was also a subcontractor in the Space Shuttle program, but it wasn't the prime contractor responsible for the entire system and mission. Boeing had much to innovate on Commercial Crew, substantially increasing schedule and cost overrun risks.

SpaceX developed the Dragon cargo resupply spacecraft before starting the Commercial Crew program, which laid the foundation for developing the human-rated version. From cargo resupply missions, SpaceX also gained design and safety process experience. Nevertheless, SpaceX

---

[21]Stephen Clark, "Boeing's Starliner Has Cost at Least Twice as Much as SpaceX's Crew Dragon," *Ars Technica*, 2024, accessed June 23, 2025, https://arstechnica.com/space/2024/07/boeing-warns-of-more-financial-losses-on-starliner-commercial-crew-program/.

[22]Marcia Smith, "Boeing's Starliner Losses Reach $2 Billion," *SpacePolicy Online.Com*, 2025, accessed August 13, 2025, https://spacepolicyonline.com/news/boeings-starliner-losses-reach-2-billion/

was still learning and innovating for the human-rated spacecraft, which resulted in overruns.

All parties to the contract—NASA, Boeing, and SpaceX—were wildly optimistic in their schedule and cost expectations. No one should be surprised, given that Boeing and SpaceX competed against each other and other companies for the contract award. They had powerful economic incentives to price and schedule aggressively to win the business. Given budget constraints from Congress and assuming contractors would overrun anyway, NASA had strong incentives to demand aggressive schedule and budget targets.

Apollo took eight years (from 1961 to 1969) to land a man on the moon, but NASA planned the first mission to occur within five years (1966). That's a 60 percent schedule overrun. The Space Shuttle program took nine years from inception to the first test flight (1972 to 1981). NASA scheduled the first flight test for 1979, so the overrun was two years, or about 29 percent. Since both the Apollo and Space Shuttle programs experienced double-digit schedule overruns and took eight to nine years to complete, all parties were optimistic that the Commercial Crew program could achieve flight certification in only three years. Alarm bells should have sounded, but unjustified optimism was alive and well and hiding in the background.

Summary

Most companies believe that poor supplier performance and technical issues are the primary causes of overruns. While these are significant factors, a key blind spot is that many other underlying habits contribute to unrealistic and unjustified optimism in baseline plans, which leads to unplanned overruns:

1. Failing to recognize and manage uncertainty.
2. Using aggressive targets to avoid overruns.
3. Tracking projects using only lagging indicators.
4. Failing to manage resource overloads.
5. Funding projects without reserves to protect against overruns.

6. Underestimating due to the planning fallacy.
7. Adopting a get-it-sold-and-keep-it-sold mindset.
8. Assessing risks optimistically.
9. Underinvesting in technical execution.
10. Exhibiting unjustified optimism.

It's essential to recognize that these blind spots are always lurking in the background, driving substantially increased risks of product market failures and overruns. Technologies like AI will help accelerate product development and reduce costs, but this only raises the bar. Eventually, everyone will use the same toolsets. While future project baselines will be shorter and less expensive, the same unjustified optimism will persist because human nature drives it. Therefore, the statistics have remained stable for many decades.

However, a pessimistic view doesn't mean we can't take action against unjustified optimism before it causes product market failures and overruns. Let's start with how to use metrics to stay on track, the subject of the next chapter.

Reader Call to Action

Review common causes of overruns. Based on the project you planned in previous Reader Call to Action sections, would you make any changes to address overrun risks related to these causes? Would you add schedule and cost reserves? Would you review your task duration estimates and increase them? Would you check other projects of equivalent complexity to see if your estimates are similar to their actual results? If you decide not to make any changes to your plan, why?

Another action is to reflect on any project in your personal or professional life that missed its schedule or budget targets. Were there more causes at play than you may have realized? What would you have done differently to anticipate and mitigate them? Did you meet the market target, despite the project being on schedule and budget? What were customers' desired results, and did the project provide a value proposition that delivered those desired results?

Lessons Learned

1. The inherent technical risks of innovation will always exist, especially when developing new technologies. There are many options to reduce these risks, including strengthening revision and configuration control, improving regulatory compliance, maintaining technical design standards, reducing resource overloads, and improving systems engineering and testing.

2. Overruns are pervasive and occur across industry, company, and government boundaries. They are often tightly integrated into organizational systems and culture, hiding in plain sight. Causes of these overruns include:

    a. Failing to recognize and manage uncertainty.

    b. Using aggressive targets to avoid overruns.

    c. Tracking projects using only lagging indicators.

    d. Failing to manage resource overloads.

    e. Funding projects without reserves to protect against overruns.

    f. Underestimating due to the planning fallacy.

    g. Adopting a get-it-sold-and-keep-it-sold mindset.

    h. Assessing risks optimistically.

    i. Underinvesting in technical execution.

    j. Exhibiting unjustified optimism.

3. Because these risks go unnoticed, they cannot be tracked or controlled and are rarely measured. Collectively, they add significant delays and costs during project execution, leading to overruns and missed commitments, brand erosion, and financial losses.

CHAPTER 7

Use Metrics to Stay on Track

We've seen why schedule and cost overruns are so common, but we don't have to accept them. This chapter and the next introduce *Targemetrics*, a discipline and toolset focused on helping you and your team prevent overruns. Instead of reacting to surprises caused by blind spots, you'll learn how to use leading and lagging metrics to spot and address issues early, managing risks before they become problems. We'll also discuss how to measure and reduce organizational resistance to project workflow, to accelerate operations and prevent overruns. Finally, many organizational processes supporting new product development projects require significant speed, quality, and cost improvements. Three mathematical ratios will help you measure the opportunities for process improvements and prioritize which processes to improve first. We will discuss these ratios later in this chapter.

Using Leading Metrics to Track Critical Activities

Leading metrics track key activities critical to project execution. For instance, a product development project often includes engineering design activities. Each engineering design activity produces one or more essential outputs, such as lines of software code, engineering drawings, prototypes, or specifications. We can use leading metrics to measure progress in generating these outputs. The best way to display leading metrics is through a cumulative line graph. See Table 7.1 and Figure 7.1.

A cumulative line accumulates each period's output. There are two cumulative lines in Figure 7.1—one for actuals and the other for the baseline plan. The two lines will be superimposed if cumulative actuals match the cumulative plan. The cumulative actuals line will be below and to the

Table 7.1 *Cumulative line chart data*

Day	Daily plan	Cumulative daily plan	Daily actuals	Cumulative daily actuals
1	0	0	0	0
2	2	2	2	2
3	1	3	1	3
4	2	5	2	5
5	2	7	1	6
6	3	10	2	8
7	2	12	2	10
8	3	15	2	12
9	3	18	1	13
10	4	22	1	14
11	4	26	2	16
12	3	29	3	19
13	4	33	3	22
14	5	38	4	26
15	5	43	5	31

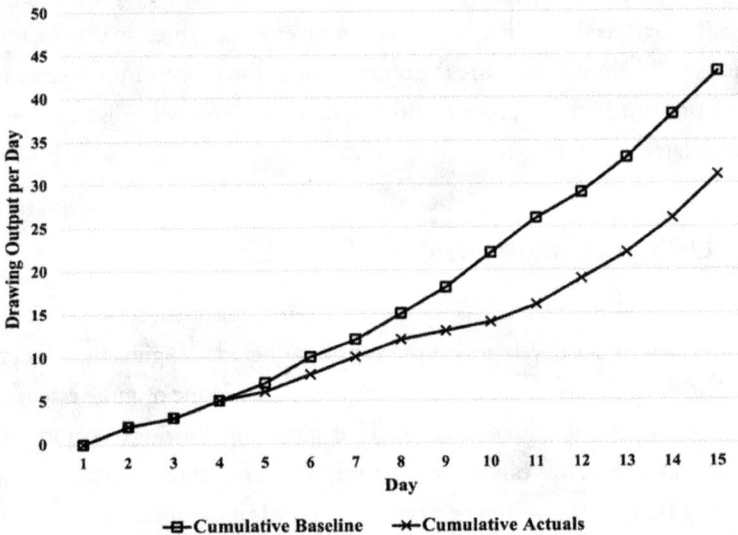

Figure 7.1 *Cumulative line chart*

right of the cumulative plan line if the project falls behind the plan. If cumulative actuals are ahead of the cumulative plan, the cumulative actuals line will be above and to the left of the cumulative plan line. Cumulative charts are sensitive to developing trends and are an excellent way to track progress on critical activities driving project performance.

Sometimes, you won't be able to identify critical activities driving your lagging indicators. For example, suppliers may not share their internal development schedules. In this case, substitute intermediate milestones for activities. Intermediate milestones are required outcomes before the final deliverable. A schedule variance for an intermediate milestone is a leading indicator because an upstream slip becomes the starting point for downstream activities.

In summary, identify the driving activities or intermediate milestones necessary to achieve a strategic outcome. Develop a performance metric for this outcome, usually a variance between the actual and planned completion dates. The metric will be a lagging indicator because it can only calculate a variance after the outcome happens. Also, develop performance metrics for each intermediate driving activity and track their progress. These are leading metrics. Every critical outcome must have at least one driving activity and associated leading metrics.

Measuring and Tracking What Slows You Down

An obvious way to prevent overruns is to accelerate project work. You can accelerate project work internally by adding resources, reducing work scope, using different technologies, leveraging AI, or finding other ways to prevent delays. You can also change the project's environment to minimize delays caused by external sources. In a sense, any source of delay, whether internal or external, is a form of resistance to project work that slows you down. A metric that can measure this resistance provides a way to determine the total opportunity for improvement to eliminate delays and accelerate projects.

A simple resistance metric (RM) is unused time capacity based on the passage of time over some reporting period.[23] Time is a perishable resource. Every day a project does not make progress is wasted time. Suppose a company tracks project progress weekly. Since a workweek lasts

_____

[23]A spreadsheet file to calculate the resistance metric for your project can be downloaded from the Resources tab at www.targemetrics.com.

five workdays based on the passage of time, the maximum time capacity for productive work, excluding overtime, is five workdays.

Suppose a project team completes two workdays of work within the current workweek, implying that three are unused. The RM is 60 percent because three-fifths of the reporting period's capacity is unused. Resistance to workflow is an excellent metric that quantifies the impact of improvement activities, enabling project work to flow more efficiently. Potential upsides of system improvements include faster delivery, fewer errors, higher product quality, fewer overruns, and improved customer satisfaction. Resistance is not a good metric for performance appraisal because it's affected by many potential sources of delays.

To calculate the RM for a project, start by calculating the resistance for each task scheduled to start or be in progress during the reporting period. Then, sum up all task-level resistance values to calculate the project-level resistance, and then again to the project portfolio level. Improvement efforts should focus on identifying and reducing the sources of highest resistance since they are generating the most significant impacts. See Table 7.2.

Columns A through C are entered by you. Column D calculates the workdays between each task's planned start date and the report date. In theory, this is the maximum number of workdays available to make progress on a task. However, fewer workdays could be available if a task's remaining duration at the start of the reporting period is less than the theoretical maximum number of workdays in Column D.

For example, the remaining duration at the beginning of the reporting period for Task 2 is 12 workdays (Column B). The duration from the planned start date to the report date is 10 workdays, as shown in Column D. This implies Task 2 has two workdays left, both of which fall into the next reporting period. It also means the maximum possible progress within the reporting period will be 10 workdays.

A task can have fewer days of work remaining than the capacity of the reporting period based on the passage of time. For example, Task 3 has three workdays remaining at the beginning of the reporting period, but there are 10 workdays from the planned start date to the report date. The maximum time capacity is three workdays because the project will

Table 7.2 *Resistance metric*

	A	B	C	D	E	F
					Report date (RD): 11/17	
Task	Planned start	Remaining duration (Workdays)	Actual progress this period	Workdays from planned start to report date (RD – A)	Max workdays through report date (Min B, D)	Resistance metric (%) (1 – (C / E))
1	11/6	10	5	10	10	50
2	11/6	12	0	10	10	100
3	11/6	3	2	10	3	33
4	11/7	8	3	9	8	63
5	11/7	2	0	9	2	100
6	11/8	10	2	8	8	75
7	11/9	10	5	7	7	29
8	11/10	1	1	6	1	0
		Total:	18		49	63

complete the rest of the task in a future reporting period. The minimum of Columns B and D, as shown in Column E, determines how much time capacity is available for work in the reporting period.

Column F calculates the RM for each task and the project. The metric is simply one minus the ratio of progress in workdays to the maximum capacity based on the passage of time, expressed as a percentage. Actual progress and maximum capacity in Columns C and E are summed across all tasks and then used in Column F to calculate the project's total resistance in percent.

A total resistance of 63 percent implies the project did not accomplish any work 63 percent of the time, or 38 minutes per working hour. Theoretically, this means there's a 63 percent opportunity to accelerate project work. Resistance occurs for various reasons, including approvals, inspections, testing, rework, mistakes, and other factors. It's unlikely you can reduce resistance to zero. However, measuring resistance is an excellent way to quantify opportunities for improvement that accelerate product development. The best way to reduce resistance is to identify the causes of delays and take action to reduce them.

Establishing Cost and Schedule Reserves

As discussed in the book's Introduction, product development cost overruns average 27 percent. Schedule overruns average 46 percent. At least 17 percent of projects are significantly worse, with cost overruns averaging 200 percent and schedule overruns averaging 70 percent. While various research studies generate different estimates, all agree that schedule and cost overruns average at least double-digit percentages.

A legitimate strategy to protect against unplanned overruns is to establish reserves before the project starts. Cost reserves should be at least 25 to 30 percent, and schedule reserves should be at least 45 to 50 percent. However, since overruns are so prevalent, it's evident that many companies don't take any action to protect themselves from overrun. Why not?

The main reason is that reserves cost money. That money must come from somewhere, either from profit, customers, lenders, or investors. Funding reserves from profit means that companies must absorb a charge against earnings and create a corresponding financial liability on the corporate balance sheet. Few executives are willing to approve voluntary profit reductions because stockholders measure their performance. They also avoid adding liabilities to the balance sheet if loan covenants exist that constrain changes to balance sheet ratios.

Customers often refuse to pay for reserves because they don't want to reward future poor performance or pay a higher price. In theory, a company could raise the money from investors or lenders, but they will have the same perceptions as customers. Market competition often generates downward price pressures, making it even more challenging to fund reserves.

The result is that management has no incentives to fund reserves against overruns. They plan for the best (no overruns) and assume the worst won't happen, despite data and history to the contrary. Operating on faith that overruns won't occur is the very definition of unjustified optimism.

In many cases, once overruns occur, executives blame project managers and their teams for poor execution, but the real issue was that the schedule and cost targets were unachievable. None of this implies that product market failures and overruns are inevitable, just that risks of them occurring are high, especially as innovation and complexity increase.

Measuring Process Improvement Opportunities

Organizational processes such as configuration management, manufacturing, engineering design, inventory management, and approval requests support product development projects. If these processes perform poorly, they can lead to overruns. One way to prevent subpar process performance from resulting in overruns is to use quantitative metrics to pinpoint opportunities for improvement. Micro-JIT (Just-In-Time) ratios are an excellent method for assessing improvement opportunities because they are operating metrics that evaluate process performance.[24]

---

[24]Richard J. Schonberger, *World Class Manufacturing Casebook: Implementing JIT and TQC* (Macmillan, 1987).

Inventory refers to the quantity of materials, transactions, or products within a system or process. Lead time is the total calendar time from the start of a process to its completion, including queues, delays, and re-work loops. Process speed represents production velocity—how fast items move through a process.

To evaluate opportunities for process improvement, you can apply three mathematical ratios: inventory relative to the number of workstations or process steps, lead time compared to value-added work content, and process speed in relation to the usage rate in the subsequent process. Each ratio offers a unique perspective on opportunities for improvement, helping to identify bottlenecks, excess inventory, and sources of waste.

Ratio of Inventory to Workstations or Process Steps

The ratio of components, assemblies, or transactions to the number of workstations or process steps helps estimate whether a process holds excessive inventory. Procuring and managing inventory costs money. Every idle job, piece of inventory, container in transit, or queue between processes contributes to an increased ratio. Therefore, it's an excellent tool for analyzing office work, including order entry, purchase orders, and engineering design.

Some companies capture substantial inventory in burn-in, curing, or approval processes. These are often excellent opportunities for process improvement, which reduces the ratio by reducing or eliminating these operations.

Ratio of Lead Time to Value-Added Work Content

The ratio of lead time to value-added work content measures how long it takes to produce a product in calendar time compared to the amount of time spent adding value. The difference represents waste since customers pay for value-added operations. Reduce or eliminate, wherever possible, any processing steps that do not add value. These steps include inspection, testing, rework, and queues. Inspection and testing do not add value because they don't transform the product; instead, they exist to prevent defective products from reaching customers.

Ratio of Process Speed to Usage Rate in the Following Process

The ratio of process speed to usage rate in the following process indicates whether a production workstation operates faster than the process or workstation it services. If it does, inventory will accumulate before the subsequent process. If all workstations operate at the pace of the slowest workstation, the entire production line will eventually function at that rate. Matching usage rate to process speed prevents excess inventory from accumulating at slower operations. If the production rate is insufficient to meet market demand, redesign the slowest workstation to increase its throughput until the next slowest workstation becomes the bottleneck. Repeat this improvement cycle to increase throughput and meet market demand.

Summary of Micro-JIT Process Improvement Ratios

The three ratios are interdependent. As the ratio of product pieces to processing steps increases, so does lead time, because there is more inventory to process. Since value-added processing time doesn't change, the ratio of lead time to value-added processing time increases. As the first two ratios increase, more inventories accumulate before the slowest processing steps, thereby increasing the processing speed-to-usage rate ratio in the subsequent process.

Ideally, all three ratios should be no greater than 1 or 2 to 1. Ratios of 3 or 4 are acceptable. It's common to observe ratios of 1,000 to 1 or higher, which present significant opportunities for process improvements that generate cost reductions, accelerate lead times, decrease yield losses, and enhance quality. These improvements help to prevent product market failures and overruns.

I once visited a supplier shipping us hundreds of optoelectronic components each month. We were there to negotiate price reductions, but they gave us a tour of the production facility before the meeting began. I utilized the micro-JIT ratios to quickly assess whether any opportunities for process improvement existed that could lower the supplier's costs, enabling them to offer us a price reduction without sacrificing their profit margins.

I immediately noticed a lot of inventory at all stages of assembly on the production floor, so I asked how many processing steps were required to build the product and how many pieces of product at every assembly level were on the floor. The process had only 25 processing steps, but it contained over 2,000 parts spread across various workstations. The inventory-to-processing steps ratio was 2,000 to 25, or 80 to 1, which revealed an 80-fold opportunity for cost reduction.

I then inquired about the total value-added processing time for the 25 processing steps previously discussed, along with the average lead time to produce one unit. They said that one unit could be constructed in 55 minutes, assuming full staffing and no delays between steps, while the average actual lead time to produce one unit was five working days. Five working days translate to 2,400 minutes of lead time, based on eight working hours per day and 60 minutes per hour. Therefore, the ratio of lead time to value-added processing time was 2,400 to 55 or 44 to 1, a 44-fold opportunity to reduce lead time for our optoelectronic product orders.

During the tour, I noticed piles of inventory in front of a few workstations. These workstations operated more slowly than the ones supplying them, so inventory accumulated at these stations over time. The supplier was running all workstations at full speed to meet efficiency targets. I recommended lowering the processing rate at the upstream workstations to match the rate of the overloaded workstations. Within a week, this change eliminated the excess inventory. System throughput was not affected because the slower workstations limited total throughput, and their process speed didn't change, but their inventory costs decreased substantially.

The ratios were easy to compute and compelling. We negotiated improved cost reduction and delivery commitments, and the supplier maintained their margins once they reduced the ratios to more reasonable levels.

You can achieve similar results for any process by simply observing, asking similar questions, and using the ratios to drive improvements.

Summary

Most companies measure and track progress toward strategic goals, such as "Reach $4 billion in revenue within four years." There's nothing wrong with measuring and monitoring strategic goals, but most companies stop there. They often don't realize that strategic progress is the result of executing other activities that drive progress toward the strategic goal. These leading activities become the starting point for lagging strategic achievements. Therefore, companies must measure and track both leading metrics and lagging metrics for each strategic goal, ensuring that they can detect and correct developing issues before they escalate and impact the achievement of the strategic goal.

Product development market failures, or conversely, how well new products meet customer needs, as well as schedule and cost overruns, are all lagging metrics. This chapter provides guidance and easily implemented metrics to track leading activities that drive strategic performance.

Metrics are not the only tools in our toolbox to prevent product market failures and overruns. We can also make policy and process changes, the subject of the following chapter.

Reader Call to Action

For the project plan you generated in the last chapter's Reader Call to Action, think about leading activities driving progress along the critical path. What metrics will you use to track the progress of leading activities? Hint: consider using a cumulative line chart like the example in Figure 7.1 to compare cumulative actuals against cumulative baseline plans.

Did you add reserves to the schedule and budget to cover unplanned overruns? If not, why? What will you do to compensate, other than hoping for the best? For example, will you add buffers to each path to absorb unplanned delays?

Will you take any actions to reduce external impacts on project performance? For example, will you measure and take actions to minimize resistance to the flow of project work?

Will you review critical processes supporting project execution? How will you measure the performance of these processes and opportunities for improvement? One way to do this is to use the three process improvement metrics described previously to measure process performance. As you make process improvements, the metrics will immediately show the amount of improvement and how much additional improvement is possible. You can measure any process this way, so if the RM is high, measure the suspect processes and let the metrics guide you on process improvements.

Lessons Learned

1. Identify and track the leading activities driving a project's schedule and cost performance. Use metrics that measure their progress to detect emerging overruns early, before they have significant impacts.
2. Assign a team and a leader to manage each leading activity. For example, if firmware development is a leading activity, a good leading metric might be the absolute and percentage variance between cumulative lines of software code and cumulative planned lines produced daily.
3. Include reserves in project baselines to protect against overruns. Cost reserves should be at least 25 to 30 percent, and schedule reserves should be at least 45 to 50 percent. You may want to add another 10 to 15 percent if your project requires significant innovation.
4. If you have room in the schedule, add time-only, non-resourced buffer tasks to the end of each path in the project's task network to act as a shock absorber against schedule overruns. When tasks along a path slip, compress the path's buffer accordingly to absorb the delay without slipping the path's scheduled end date.
5. Organizational inertia is a hidden resistance to project workflow that slows projects and contributes to overruns. You can measure resistance and use it to guide process improvements.
6. Three metrics can quickly reveal improvement opportunities in any process: the ratio of lead time to work content, the ratio of process speed to the usage rate in the following process, and the ratio of inventory or transactions to the number of workstations. Ideal values for all three ratios are 1 or 2 to 1. Good ratios are 2 or 3 to 1. Much higher ratios of 1,000 or more are typical.

CHAPTER 8

Prevent Overruns with Process Changes

We discussed how metrics are essential indicators of process performance. However, we haven't yet discussed how to modify processes to enhance their performance, as measured by the metrics. Metrics and process changes are complementary. They're covered separately because metrics are tools to measure performance, while process changes affect performance directly.

Let History Be Your Guide: Reference Class Forecasting

A common blind spot in estimation is neglecting the experience and evidence of others, which leads to underestimating the complexity and scope of work, ultimately causing overruns. External comparisons are crucial for ensuring realistic and achievable estimates because they serve as a reality check against internal influences, such as incentives and competition, that can foster unjustified optimism.

There are several ways to perform outside comparisons: RCF and benchmarking. RCF uses historical data to predict a future outcome by looking at a reference class of similar projects. In contrast, benchmarking compares performance metrics against industry performance or standards to improve processes. RCF is more predictive and helpful for preventing unjustified optimism in forecasts.

For example, a manufacturer planning a new technology platform development project might use RCF to estimate the schedule and budget by analyzing data from similar projects in the past, both internally and across the industry. The same manufacturer might use benchmarking to identify state-of-the-art user safety standards and trends to ensure new products meet market safety requirements.

You may not need to use RCF if you have much experience with your forecasting subject matter. For example, a vertically integrated company may have sufficient knowledge and experience manufacturing a product to make accurate forecasts. In contrast, a horizontally integrated company buys most of what it needs rather than building internally, so it may have less knowledge and experience and, therefore, will tend to forecast more optimistically.

Conducting Project Management Reviews

Project Management Reviews are essential tools to prevent overruns. They engage executive management in discussions with project teams to review current and projected project performance, issues, decisions, and risks. In many startups, the CEO runs a daily or weekly all-hands meeting to discuss the status of one or two strategic priorities. The all-hands meeting works well in a startup environment, but it doesn't scale as the organization grows because too many people are involved. Eventually, the company needs a structured Project Management Review (PMR) process.

Schedule PMR meetings at least monthly. You can plan them more frequently, but a monthly schedule is usually best because most accounting systems only generate cost data monthly. Scheduling meetings quarterly is generally a bad idea because the meetings will not keep up with the high rate of change on most projects. For the meetings to be effective, executives, project managers, functional managers, and core team leads should attend all PMR meetings.

A PMR does not have to be long, complex, or tedious. Except for the largest and most complex projects, all relevant content should fit into a four-part, one-page presentation slide called a quad chart. See Figure 8.1 on the following page.

The top-left section lists overview information for meeting participants, especially those unfamiliar with the project. The top-right quadrant provides project financial information. The bottom-left quadrant shows the project's schedule in tabular format. Each row is a key project milestone. The bottom-right quadrant describes critical constraints slowing progress.

The data in the top-right financial quadrant often includes EV data like EAC, EV, Cost Performance Index (CPI), and Schedule Performance Index (SPI). While a detailed discussion of EV is beyond the scope of

Report Date:	1/7/2026		**Current Budget:** $325,000
Project Name:	"Enterprise"		**Total Budget:** $1,500,000
Project Number:	105364		**Actual Cost:** $350,000
Tracking Number:	A2537		**Estimate at Complete (EAC):** $1,600,000
Product:	Advanced circular saw		**Projected Overrun:** $100,000
Customer/Market:	Professional woodworkers		**Earned Value:** $300,000
Market Launch:	May 2026		**Cost Performance Index (CPI):** 0.86
			Schedule Performance Index (SPI): 0.92

Milestone	Baseline	Actual or Outlook	Variance (days) ("-" is late)	**Critical Constraints Slowing Progress**
Kick-off	1/15/2026	1/22/2026	-7	• The project team was understaffed by two engineers. This is the main cause of the overruns and schedule slips.
Design	1/31/2026	2/07/2026	-7	
Prototype	2/28/2026	3/15/2026	-14	• Manufacturing Engineering is not yet a constraint but will be once higher-priority factory upgrades start.
Launch	5/15/2026	6/15/2026	-31	

Instructions:

1. Describe the project (top-left)
2. Summarize current financials (top-right)
3. Show progress results against plan for critical milestones (bottom-left)
4. Discuss critical constraints that slow progress (bottom-right).

Figure 8.1 PMR quad chart

this book, the EAC is a current forecast of total spending on the project by the time it's complete. EV is the work completed to date, expressed in dollars. The CPI is the ratio of EV to actual cost to date. If the CPI equals 0.86, then $0.86 of work was accomplished for every dollar spent on the project to date. CPI is therefore a measure of cost efficiency. Similarly, the SPI is the ratio of EV to planned cost to date. If the SPI is 0.92, then for every dollar the project planned to spend, it accomplished $0.92 of work. The SPI is therefore a measure of schedule efficiency.

The milestone table in the bottom-left quadrant is critical. It should list all critical project performance milestones, especially those in the contract. The data columns show baseline schedule dates, current outlook (if the milestone date is in the future) or actual completion date (if the milestone date is in the past), and the difference (variance) in days between the two. If the variance is unfavorable, then the milestone is behind schedule. The variance is a direct measure of progress.

The meeting agenda may include additional topics like a significant project success, an important issue or concern, or a critical upcoming milestone. You can add another page or two as appropriate. A frequent error is to troubleshoot technical issues during the meeting. Keep discussions high-level and brief. Assign actions to schedule separate meetings for detailed discussions, including developing recovery plans.

Simplifying Internal Approvals

Internal approvals are one of the biggest blind spots in product development and a significant source of project delays and frustrations for project teams. As organizations grow, management typically adds more and more approvals to internal workflows. These approvals are usually in response to mistakes or to review newly identified risks. Each approval requires time for the approver to review and then approve, disapprove, or hold the request pending more information. Wait time may exist between when the approval request arrives in the approver's queue and when the approver reviews it.

In general, requesters are more knowledgeable about the approval request's subject matter than the approvers, which forces the requester to prepare additional documentation to educate the approver and justify the request. Approvals multiply because growing organizations tend to centralize, management layers increase, and financial decisions become more risky.

Because time is critical for approval decisions, requestors often expedite the approval chain with e-mails, phone calls, text messages, and meeting requests to overcome queues and increase pressure on the approvers to decide more quickly. Expediting wastes time and money because its sole purpose is to overcome inertia in organizational approval processes. Labor and cycle time invested in approvals do not add value for customers.

The most common reason companies add approvals is to prevent past mistakes that resulted in significant financial losses. However, the cure can be worse than the disease. Executives often forget to consider how frequently mistakes will occur in the future. An approval is equivalent to a 100 percent inspection. If the probability of the error is low, say 1 percent, then the other 99 percent of items processed without errors must also go through the same approval process. *This wastes time and money because the items are already error-free.*

Approvals are much more expensive than most people realize. The numbers for a representative scenario tell the story.

Assume a processing mistake was made on a parts order, costing the company $50,000 in losses. Also, assume 1,000 parts orders are processed monthly, and the ordering mistake occurs twice yearly. Management recognizes the mistakes and resulting losses, and in response, adds a new approval process for all parts orders exceeding $25,000. Furthermore, 25 percent of parts orders are over $25,000. Approvers average 15 minutes to review and approve or reject each approval request. Salaries of approvers average $250,000 per year. Salaries of approval requesters average $150,000 per year.

Since the loss from a single mistake is $50,000 and is likely to occur twice yearly, the average annual loss will be $100,000 or $500,000 over five years. As a result, the new approval must cost less than $500,000 over five years to justify adding it; otherwise, the company would be better off economically if the mistakes were allowed to continue. Of course, it would be the least expensive to change the parts ordering process to prevent errors. Still, we are considering only the costs and benefits of adding an approval for this analysis.

The cost of adding the approval is straightforward to estimate. Since 1,000 orders are processed monthly, and 25 percent are for over $25,000,

250 orders must be routed through the approval process monthly. The approver's labor rate assumes a standard 40-hour workweek and three weeks of vacation annually, as shown in (1):

$$\$127.55 \text{ per hour} = \$250,000 \div \tag{1}$$
$$(49 \text{ weeks per year} \times 40 \text{ hours per workweek})$$

Since it takes 15 minutes for the approver to review and approve each approval request, the labor cost is one-fourth of $127.55 per hour or $31.89 per order. However, this is only a payroll cost. It doesn't include allocations for fixed costs like fringe benefits, overhead, or General and Administrative (G&A) expenses. Total allocations are often between three and four times the payroll labor rate. Assume a multiplier of $3.5\times$. The labor cost to approve each order is in (2):

$$\$111.61 \text{ per approval} = \$250,000 \div \tag{2}$$
$$(49 \text{ weeks} \times 40 \text{ hours per week}) \times 3.5 \text{ Allocations Multipler} \div 4 \text{ hours}$$

The labor cost per approval in (2) includes only the approver's labor. Other labor costs include the requester's time spent generating documentation to explain and justify the approval request. This documentation is usually more detailed than if the order didn't require formal approvals.

Assume the requester spends one hour preparing the additional documentation and expediting the request as it winds through the approval loop. The additional labor cost is in (3):

$$\$267.86 \text{ per approval} = \$150,000 \div (49 \text{ weeks} \times \tag{3}$$
$$40 \text{ hours per week}) \times 3.5 \text{ Allocations Multipler} \div 1 \text{ hour}$$

Total labor cost per approval is therefore $379.47. The total labor cost for 250 orders per month is $379.47 $\times$ 250, which equals $94,867.50 per month, $1,138,410 per year, and $5,692,050 over five years. Adding only one approval costs the company over $1 million annually, *forever*, which is *double* the $500,000 annual cost of doing nothing and allowing the ordering mistakes to continue. Adding the new approval may prevent the errors, but the approval cost isn't worth it. The cure is worse than the disease.

Of course, a third, better option is to change procedures and provide training to prevent mistakes. Prevention at the source eliminates the need for approvals while also eliminating the costs of errors. *Save approvals for important risk decisions, not as an after-the-fact inspection to screen out errors.*

New approvals quickly fade from view because they become part of the organization's system. Employees working in the system are aware of the extra work and stress that approvals create. However, most employees will only challenge management if they believe management will listen and simplify or remove the approvals.

Besides labor costs, approvals also increase cycle time. Cycle time is the total elapsed time it takes for one unit of work to move through a single process step or the entire process, from start to finish. In our parts ordering example, cycle time is the elapsed time from creating a parts order to placement with the supplier.

Assume approval requests sit in the approver's inbox for half a workday (this is generous; a couple of days is common). Also, assume each order takes two workdays for standard processing, excluding the additional approval.

Since 250 orders each month require an additional approval, and it takes one-half of a workday to process the approval, the cycle time will increase by 125 workdays monthly. The total monthly cycle time is in (4):

$$625 \text{ days} = (250 \text{ orders} \times \tfrac{1}{2} \text{ day per order}) + \\ (250 \text{ orders} \times 2 \text{ days per order}) \tag{4}$$

Adding only one approval increased the parts order processing cycle time by 25 percent (125 divided by 500). *The additional cycle time results in a slower process.* No one plans for this impact because it's not visible in the system, so schedule overruns will occur unless the procurement function compensates by placing orders earlier or convincing suppliers to deliver faster. For the former, procurement functions usually must wait for project teams to provide specifications, statements of work, and other information before placing the order, so there are limited opportunities to place orders earlier. For the latter, competition usually ensures suppliers are already trying to deliver as fast as possible. For these reasons, the cycle time increase will likely show up as schedule overruns and permanently longer new product development cycles.

There are additional unplanned impacts. When approval requesters spend time preparing documentation and expediting approval requests, they're not working on value-added activities for customers. Assume the system loses one hour of skilled labor to execute value-added activities for customers. For 250 orders monthly, this is a value-added labor capacity decrease of 250 hours per month. A standard Full Time Equivalent (FTE) is one person working 40 hours per week for 49 weeks per year, including three weeks of vacation, as shown in (5):

$$163.33 \text{ hours per month per FTE} = 40 \text{ hours per week} \\ \times 49 \text{ weeks per year} \div 12 \text{ months per year} \qquad (5)$$

If we divide 250 labor hours monthly by 163 labor hours per FTE per month, rounded, the result is about 1.5 FTE per month of lost labor capacity. The total value of the annual value-added labor capacity loss is in (6):

$$\$787,500 \text{ per year} = \$12,500 \text{ monthly salary} \times 3.5 \text{ Allocations} \\ \text{Multiplier} \times 1.5 \text{ FTE per month} \times 12 \text{ months per year} \qquad (6)$$

The result in (6) shows that one approval costs about $787,500 annually of lost value-added labor capacity. These people could be taking care of customers and generating revenue instead of managing internal approvals. No one in executive management pays attention to these impacts because there are no explicit measurements. And don't forget, this $787,500 value-added labor capacity loss is on top of the labor costs to process the approvals, which is over $1.1 million annually, for a total cost of over $1.9 million annually. Over five years, the total cost of adding just this one approval would be $9.5M, an eye-popping figure!

It doesn't matter if the cost assumptions in this example are off by even orders of magnitude. The point of the analysis is to show that it's feasible to do back-of-the-envelope estimates to assess the magnitude of the problem and make it visible, and to show that the cost and cycle time impacts will accumulate and become far larger than you would typically expect.

No wonder large companies tend to become expensive, slow, and unresponsive. Standard corporate financial reports do not directly measure the impacts of approvals on costs, so companies often compensate for increases in bureaucracy by hiring more people to do the extra work. Hiring more people, especially executives, tends to add even more approvals, adding to the burdens.

Organizations add more and more approvals to reduce perceived risks and prevent mistakes. Only some executives bother to determine the cost impacts of their decisions. Many don't even think about it, much less take any action. For all practical purposes, they effectively assume approvals are free because no one does a return on investment analysis as described above. Since demand increases as the price plummets to zero, naturally, there will be an ever greater number of approvals.

After-the-fact inspections are pervasive in business, despite quality assurance experts proving that they don't work. Examples of after-the-fact inspections include receiving inspections of incoming materials, production inspections, approvals, and reviews of work already done. Eliminating after-the-fact inspections, such as approvals, represents a massive opportunity for cost reductions, cycle time improvements, and value-added labor capacity increases, without additional hiring or financial investments.

Another lesson learned is that the cost impacts of most decisions are relatively easy to estimate with simple math and basic knowledge of costs and probabilities. The estimates can be approximate, especially for recurring transactions where the costs multiply quickly. The point of this exercise is that if you place a price on the decision by calculating approximate cost impacts, the right choices will be made based on relative value, instead of on subjective opinions.

Strengthening Project Scope Management

Unplanned scope changes are a blind spot that few companies track, leading to many schedule and cost overruns. They occur in many ways. For example, projects sometimes burn through approved contract funding, but the team continues working. Working beyond contract funding is risky because the customer is not obligated to pay for the work.

Sometimes, a customer requests unplanned work without formal approval through a contractual change order. If the supplier proceeds, the customer is not obligated to pay for the job. If the unplanned work results in a schedule slip, the customer can hold the supplier responsible because it was not contractually approved. Suppliers often track unapproved costs and submit a request for reimbursement later. This request is called a claim. Submitting after-the-fact claims is risky, because if the customer negotiates the claim down or refuses to pay for all or part of the work, the supplier must absorb the loss, possibly causing a cost overrun.

Determining whether unplanned work is in or out of scope depends on the contract's terms and conditions. Management starts by referring to language within what's called the four corners of the contract, meaning language that is in the agreement, regarding the unplanned work. Suppose the contract does not explicitly specify how to handle the unplanned work. In that case, they will review other tangible evidence, like e-mails or text messages, as to the parties' original intent.

The next step is determining if the contract specifies a dispute clause, which describes dispute resolution procedures, including escalating to executive management on both sides. If executives fail to reach an agreement, the matter goes to mediation, arbitration, litigation, or other methods.

Project scope management is a consistent weakness of project teams. Project managers want to make customers happy, but often overlook the risks associated with accepting unplanned work, particularly the potential for overruns. For example, because customers don't pay for changes they didn't contractually approve (even if customers request them), their satisfaction is lower because a price defines value. Since the price is zero, the change has no value.

If a company's gross margin is 50 percent, then each dollar spent on unplanned, unpaid work requires at least $2 of additional revenue to compensate for the loss. To generate more revenue, the company must win more orders. Winning more orders may be difficult because most order targets are already aggressive and have a relatively low likelihood of success.

If the impact of a change is small and the project manager has sufficient schedule and budget reserve available, the project manager may want to accept an unplanned change request as a freebie. To attach value to the change, it would be a good idea to keep a log of all freebies provided and what the price would have been for each freebie. Communicate this to customers periodically. The idea is to set up a future quid pro quo. For example, "I gave you three freebies worth $50,000 in the last three months, so how about you work with me on the current issue?"

Some customers are skilled negotiators who demand additional features at no extra cost. They often use language in their demands regarding what the supplier could have, would have, or should have done in a particular situation. Such assertions are a dead giveaway to these hardball negotiating tactics because they are self-serving opinions, not reality.

Training project and contract managers on customer management and negotiation skills is worth the time and effort. Inadequate project scope management often goes unnoticed. Many commercial courses are available in project scope management, contract management, and negotiation. A simple online search will turn up options.

Improving Supply Chain Management

Poor supplier performance is a significant source of schedule and cost overruns. Most companies are aware of this, but in the author's experience, many supply chain management organizations are understaffed and tend to focus more on purchase transactions and supply contracts than on preventing overruns. Therefore, it's essential to track leading metrics of supplier performance to provide early warning of potential supplier delays. Most companies measure supplier performance only with lagging metrics, resulting in the discovery of delivery delays after they occur, which is too late.

The best way to prevent supplier overruns is to identify critical driving activities in the supplier's process or at the supplier's suppliers and their associated leading metrics. However, suppliers are often reluctant to provide visibility to customers on their internal processes, especially on their supply chains. If customers see significant risks, they frequently attempt to micromanage the supplier, which can be highly disruptive and expensive. It doesn't help that many companies take an adversarial approach to managing their supply chain, using heavy-handed negotiating tactics to force recurring price reductions or onerous delivery terms on their suppliers. An antagonistic relationship does not encourage suppliers to invest in the relationship or be transparent about order and development status.

Despite these obstacles, it's essential to track supplier project performance often. Many companies track supplier performance monthly, which is inadequate. The reporting frequency should be at least weekly, plus monthly PMR meetings. Weekly reporting should focus on the progress of critical driving activities using leading metrics. Weekly and monthly reports should follow the PMR quad chart format discussed in the previous chapter. Do the same for supplier PMR meetings.

Investing in Technical Execution

Poor technical execution, especially in new technology development projects, is often a significant cause of overruns. The best way to prevent design iterations and associated schedule delays is to capture and preserve core standards of technical excellence while still allowing for creativity, innovation, and fast execution. Organizations must invest in continuous improvement of technical policies, standards, procedures, tools, and training.

A key blind spot is that many organizations don't invest enough in their technical staff, primarily relying on their academic education and on-the-job training. Senior technical staff are often so busy that they don't have enough time to mentor junior staff, and they are frequently severely multitasked, creating bottlenecks and substantially increasing the risks of overruns.

Companies often view critical technical support functions, such as configuration management, as costs to minimize rather than as essential resources for swift and effective technical execution. Additionally, other important tasks, such as testing, systems engineering, process analysis, process control, supplier engineering, and tolerance analysis, tend to be underfunded in bids, proposals, and annual budget planning.

Using AI to Accelerate Product Development

Artificial Intelligence (AI) technology is a promising tool for accelerating product development. The technology excels at time-consuming tasks that often involve reviewing documentation and trial-and-error learning. The user still must provide human expertise to frame the problem, but AI can provide an accurate solution in a fraction of the time it would take with other methods.

For example, AI applications such as ChatGPT, Chatsonic, Claude, DeepSeek (a Chinese-owned company), Google Gemini, Microsoft Copilot, and Perplexity AI can help developers significantly accelerate their learning of new tasks. The AI software landscape is changing rapidly, so this list isn't meant to be exhaustive. Say that a developer needs to remove a background from an image, but has never done so before. The usual approach is to do an internet search for an app that removes backgrounds from images, and hope that the software's user manual is available online or that someone has created a YouTube how-to video. This iterative search process can be time-consuming.

However, with an AI application, the user can simply ask the software how to complete the task, and it responds with context-specific, step-by-step instructions. If any steps are unclear, the user can request clarification in a dialogue. In the author's experience, these instructions have been remarkably accurate and precise.

AI applications can also assist product developers in creative tasks, such as brainstorming ideas, developing storyboards, designing and testing product concepts, and writing engaging ad copy. The tool simplifies research by providing specific answers to prompts, eliminating the need to sift through a list of possible results. The prompts can be iterative depending on the AI tool's initial answers.

AI tools can write software code. As of this writing, the generated code may not be as efficient as expertly human-generated code; however, this gap is likely to close as AI technology advances. Already, many developers are starting with AI-generated code and then modifying it for efficiency and performance, a much faster and less iterative process than starting from scratch without the aid of AI.

Existing software applications aren't standing still. They're responding to the AI threat by integrating AI capabilities directly into their applications. For example, CAD tools can rapidly and automatically convert new product conceptual models into detailed design models without human intervention while also analyzing the designs for manufacturability and testability.

There's no doubt AI can produce excellent results. Product developers should leverage AI to accelerate product development, increase productivity, and reduce risk. However, AI isn't perfect, and there are caveats. AI is only as good as the prompts you ask it. The user provides context and frames the problem that the AI tool will solve. It's up to the user to determine if the answer is helpful and accurate. If you use AI to conduct market or other research, be careful to ask AI for its sources and ensure that what it tells you is accurate.

The models AI uses rely on aggregated data from across the Internet, which can amplify historical trends, perpetuate biases, and average out interesting and relevant outliers in the data. Therefore, consider background biases when evaluating AI's output on intangibles such as product design, aesthetics, customer preferences, and usability.

Finally, while AI has great potential to accelerate product development, it should not be expected to eliminate overruns and product market failures. As discussed in previous chapters, human habits and behaviors drive unjustified optimism that causes most overruns and product market failures. Economic incentives such as competition, job security, bonuses, and pressure to perform will remain. While AI may reduce development mistakes and, therefore, the number of unplanned design iterations, people will still be systematically optimistic in their estimates. As a result, the material in this book will remain relevant for a long time.

Summary

As previously discussed, unjustified optimism is pervasive throughout all stages of the product development life cycle. One of the best ways to prevent unjustified optimism is to learn from history through reference class forecasting. What have you or others done that is roughly similar in size and complexity to your product development effort? How long did it take, and how much did it cost? If your estimates are much more aggressive than the historical data, *what makes your team so much better?*

How are you managing your product development process? Do you hold monthly PMR meetings, as discussed in this chapter? If you don't, you'll miss developing issues because people have incentives to avoid looking bad in front of the boss, which makes them tend to minimize current problems and forecast future progress optimistically.

What about reducing internal approvals, which are a costly way to reduce risk and often radically slow down product development? Internal approvals usually operate in the background as part of the system. Once they go in, they rarely come out unless executive management makes a concerted effort to do cost–benefit analyses on each approval, which, in the author's experience, is seldom done.

Supplier overruns frequently lead to significant delays in development projects. Do you have enough people to manage the supply chain beyond simply placing orders and tracking deliveries? Suppliers have the same incentives as your project teams to be optimistic, so they report positive news to maintain good relationships with customers.

Project teams often struggle with controlling project scope. Customers request additional services, new features, and support, but they typically prefer not to pay for them. Project teams often believe they must keep customers happy and satisfy them, so they sometimes agree to do unplanned, unpaid work, which leads to overruns. Marketing and executive management often force unplanned scope changes, sometimes without realizing it. *Do you have a documented change management system that everyone follows to control project scope?*

Are you investing in technical education and leveraging state-of-the-art design and simulation tools to enhance product quality, reduce product development cycle times, and prevent mistakes that lead to overruns? Are you leveraging AI? If not, your competitors will.

Many resource managers struggle to optimize throughput and productivity when total demand on their resources exceeds capacity, resulting in unplanned overruns. The following chapter provides metrics and analytical tools to solve resource overallocation problems quickly.

Reader Call to Action

For the project you've been working on from previous Reader Calls to Action, think about the environment in which the project operates. How does the organization determine schedules and budgets for bids and proposals? Is there a systematic approach to using RCF as a reality check to ensure that schedule and cost estimates are realistic?

How will the project's progress be reviewed with management to ensure project performance, accountability, responsibility, and leadership? Will there be a PMR process?

What recurring approvals are required as the project executes? Does every purchase requisition go through extended approvals? If so, why? Is each approval worth its cost?

How will the project team implement scope and contract management for the project? The challenge is to ensure only approved, funded work is performed by the project team and charged to the project. Executing unfunded, unplanned work without change orders generates overruns that customers are rarely willing to pay for.

Supplier delivery delays are a frequent source of product development overruns and product quality issues. Are you reviewing suppliers' progress in weekly status meetings and monthly deep-dive PMR meetings? Are you identifying and tracking key activities driving each supplier's schedule?

Technical issues are significant causes of overruns. How are you mitigating technical risks, including training and improving technical policies, procedures, design standards, and tools?

If you're not using AI, look hard at it because your competition will. How will you integrate AI tools into process changes to accelerate product development?

Lessons Learned

1. Let history be your guide when estimating schedules and costs. What have you or others done of a similar size and complexity? Encourage contrarian views. Ask team members and unbiased third parties for feedback on estimates.
2. If your estimates are more aggressive than historical trends, why would you perform so much better?
3. Institute a monthly systematic PMR process to review the progress of all projects and discuss decisions, issues, and risks.
4. Simplify internal approvals. One approval can cost millions over the long term and not add value for customers. Approvals slow down decisions, add bureaucracy, consume staff capacity, and increase risks of overruns.
5. Tighten project and contract scope management. Executing unplanned work without change orders to fund them generates overruns that customers rarely pay for.
6. Tighten supply chain tracking and control. Delivery is far more critical than cost reductions because supplier delivery slips can unexpectedly generate overruns. Review supplier progress weekly with monthly PMR meetings. Identify and track key activities driving the supplier's schedule.
7. To prevent overruns, continuously review and improve engineering standards, policies, procedures, tools, and training. Many companies underinvest in systems engineering, tolerance analysis, configuration and revision control, quality assurance, mission assurance, and process analysis and control.
8. AI has great potential to accelerate all phases of new product development. Still, it won't eliminate human habits and behaviors that cause unjustified optimism in schedule, cost, and market commitments.

CHAPTER 9

Manage Resource Capacity

We've seen how combining quantitative metrics and process changes can improve performance and prevent overruns. But that's only part of the solution. We also need to address resource bottlenecks, which are a consistent cause of overruns. Resource bottlenecks are neither good nor bad, they exist. Most organizations are very much aware of resource bottlenecks, but their blind spot is not systematically managing and reducing them to prevent overruns.

Using Project-Based Organizational Structures

Organizational structure significantly impacts product development effectiveness and efficiency. The functional structure and the project-based structure are two fundamental organizational building blocks. As a company and its project portfolio grow, these building blocks may be combined in different ways to support efficient and effective project execution.

A functional organization manages *inputs*, including people, expertise, materials, methods, processes, infrastructure, facilities, or equipment. In contrast, a project-based organization manages *outputs*, including projects, products, or services. Neither organization is better or worse than the other. They are both needed, but for different purposes.

For example, functional organizations are the primary structure for groups that support product development or executive management. Standard functions that support executive management include Human Resources, Accounting, Finance, and Legal. Those that support new product development projects may consist of Design Engineering, Quality Assurance, Manufacturing, Test Engineering, and Configuration Management, among many others. You can usually tell what resources and expertise they manage based on their names. Functional organizations are permanent structures. They hire, train, and manage people with similar expertise, develop standard policies and procedures, and build capabilities to support project execution.

In contrast, project organizations are temporary because projects have defined starts and finishes. Functions assign resources to projects full-time or part-time. Part-time assignments often lead to multitasking, which can result in overruns if too many projects start with the available resources. Some companies organize around their projects, especially if the projects are significant and will last for years. People may formally report to project managers who manage the project teams. However, in most cases, people report to their function's manager, who assigns them to projects as required. An important characteristic of project teams is that they are multidisciplinary, composed of whatever functional expertise is required to execute the project.

The simplest structure is purely functional, where all functional leaders report directly to the general manager or CEO. Startups and small companies often use a functional structure to organize product development. They rarely have separate project managers or project organizations. The founder runs the business and makes all strategic and product management decisions. The organization usually has only one or two new products under development because of limited resources and funding. Each functional manager has project management authority for their portion of the project work. The decision-making flow is vertical, so a separate project-based organization isn't needed.

As the company grows, it discovers that the vertical flow of communication and the increase in multitasking limit the effectiveness of functional organizations. The vertical structure hinders cross-functional and horizontal teamwork and decision-making, resulting in mistakes and overruns. Eventually, the organization evolves into a lightweight project structure.

The lightweight project structure is typical in organizations with approximately 100 to 250 employees and a project portfolio of five to 10 contracts or more. In this structure, project managers are separated from functional organizations but possess limited decision-making authority. Their primary responsibilities include tracking progress, following up on issues and risks, serving as the point of contact with customers and executive management, preparing status reports, and leading project review meetings. While many decisions remain vertical, some may flow horizontally.

The lightweight structure supports increased complexity better than the functional organization, but not by much. Eventually, project performance lags again because the mostly vertical flow of decisions still needs to be faster and cannot keep up with the higher complexity of a larger, more diverse project portfolio. The structure must evolve again into a balanced matrix.

The balanced matrix structure seeks to resolve conflicts regarding decision-making authority by sharing that authority among all parties. While shared authority may appear to create satisfaction among everyone, the reality is quite different since no single individual is in charge. Lack of authority and responsibility leads to constant negotiations over routine decisions. Deadlocks frequently arise, pushing decisions up to a level with the authority to make them. As a result, high-level decision-makers are bottlenecks, becoming preoccupied with lower-level decisions that divert their attention from their primary, higher-level responsibilities. Consequently, lower-level individuals are left waiting for decisions, leading to increased delays in all areas. No single person, except the CEO, is accountable or responsible for these outcomes.

Management eventually realizes that the balanced matrix structure isn't working. However, the organization is too complex to revert to functional or lightweight models. Thus, it evolves again into a heavyweight project management structure that forms separate teams to execute each project. The project manager leads the team and is responsible for the project schedule, cost, and technical performance. The project manager is like a mini-GM. Functional managers assign people to staff the team and provide technical leadership and support as needed.

Team members report to their functional manager for compensation and performance appraisal, and indirectly to the project manager. Project managers sometimes report to a dedicated project management function called the PMO, or Project Management Office. The PMO runs product development projects, develops project management policies and procedures, and hires, trains, and develops project managers.

The heavyweight project management structure is stable and scalable. However, resource multitasking often remains a problem, as project managers and team members typically serve on multiple project teams. Many organizations fail to provide their project teams with adequate training in leadership, project management, and account management. Prolonged learning curves can lead to mistakes, resulting in overruns. Furthermore, many companies neglect to standardize how to structure and organize project teams. Core teams composed of standardized roles are critical to an effective project management system.

Using Core Teams Composed of Standard Roles

The conventional approach to forming project teams is to staff them with people from support functions. However, team members are on their own to figure out how to work together. The ad hoc approach doesn't work well because it defaults to the experiences and knowledge of the team members. Senior people may make the right decisions, but junior people often need more guidance. The company should establish standards for structuring project teams with stable, core roles so new teams don't have to reinvent the wheel. Individuals may transfer into and out of teams, but the roles they play on the teams don't change.

Core teams are typically composed of five standard roles:

- Project Manager (PM)
- Technical Manager (TM)
- Manufacturing Manager (MM)
- Quality Manager (QM)
- Supply Chain Manager (SCM)

The PM role leads the project team and is responsible for project cost, schedule, and technical performance. The PM is also the project's primary contact with customers and executive management.

The TM is responsible for developing the product or service that the project delivers. This role is sometimes called the Project Engineer (PE) or

Cognizant Engineer (CE). The TM is responsible for product design and leading the technical team. This person is the primary technical POC for the project, including for customers.

The MM is responsible for developing the product's manufacturing process, including assembly, integration, and testing. This role may differ for services or software. The TM and MM work together to ensure the product design is manufacturable and works properly in the intended application.

The QM is responsible for configuration management, compliance, and quality assurance and acts as the team's conscience to ensure compliance with corporate, customer, and regulatory requirements. The QM also reviews and certifies test results and implements inspection and other quality assurance requirements. The most crucial responsibility of the QM is to catalyze problem-solving and ensure the team does not make bad decisions, such as accepting poor product quality.

The SCM is responsible for the project's supply chain. The SCM's primary focus is to ensure supplier performance and be the point of contact between the project team, the company's procurement organization, and suppliers. The PM may decide not to staff the SCM role if the project does not require outside materials.

These five roles are the essential elements of an effective project core team. It's common for individuals assigned to these roles to work on multiple projects, but this is a bad idea because multitasking doesn't work. It only causes delays, mistakes, and overruns. Core team roles are all *leadership* roles meant to be filled by senior people with appropriate experience and expertise.

Ideally, a core team should meet at least weekly to review project progress and address issues. The PM should lead this meeting, with the TM as backup if the PM can't be available. Because work occurs one day at a time, the team should also hold daily early morning tag-up meetings, ideally for no more than 15 minutes, to review critical actions for the day and the results of key actions from the previous day. Daily tag-ups and weekly team meetings ensure that the team temporarily stops what it is doing to communicate with each other. The focus of all meetings is on discussing results against plans, not activities.

Using a Workload Metric to Optimize Resource Workloads

A resource pool is a group of similar resources whose workload a company must manage. These resources may be materials, methods, machines, people, or a combination. They may also be employees or contractors, on-site or off-site, part-time or full-time. Resource pools are standard in virtually every organization. For example, a resource pool could be a test engineering department comprising 10 test engineers and a manager, along with test engineering policies, procedures, standards, processes, and equipment. The department is responsible for designing, installing, configuring, and maintaining production test equipment. Similarly, the HR and accounting departments are also resource pools.

Most resource pool managers struggle to optimize resource productivity across their entire project workload. They often accept, or are forced to accept, more work than their resource pools can handle, resulting in reduced throughput and delays for users waiting for their projects to start or complete. As new work arrives at a resource pool, the manager must decide when to release it without overloading the pool's resources. Most managers do this ad hoc, without any systematic or mathematical logic in their thinking. An innovative solution involves using a workload metric that indicates when to release work to the resource pool.[25]

To calculate the metric, we need to know the workload on the resource pool's most heavily used resource (its bottleneck), the number of resources in the resource pool, and the resource pool's average project length.

The workload is the average number of tasks, or labor hours, assigned to each resource. You can use either one, just be consistent. If the workload is asymmetric, such as having a large number of short tasks mixed with a small number of long tasks, use the median instead of the average to prevent data skew resulting from outliers.

---

[25]James R. Holt, and Robin Clark, "Finding the Sweet Spot in Resource Workload," *ISE Magazine* 50, no. 4 (2018): 32–36, accessed June 23, 2025, https://extendsim.com/images/downloads/papers/general-ise201804.pdf.

The resource pool size is the number of individuals with comparable skills, similar machines, or other similar resources performing the work.

The average project length is the average number of tasks per project or the average project duration, typically in working days.

The workload metric is simple to calculate. It divides the workload by the number of resources in the resource pool and then divides this result by the average project length. The final value measures the portion of an average project held in the resource pool's backlog. For example, if the resource pool's average workload is 20 tasks, the resource pool contains 10 resources, and the average project length is five tasks, then the workload metric's value is 0.40, or 40% (20 tasks divided by 10 resources divided by five tasks). In other words, the average workload on the resource pool is 40% of the average project length, or two tasks. Expressing workload as a percentage of the resource pool's average project length helps to visualize how much of the project load is sitting in backlog waiting for resources to become available.

In the example, the absolute number of tasks waiting for service appears low at only two tasks, but in percentage terms, it's 40 percent of the average project length. A 40% backlog is significant, and users would not be happy waiting for their projects to start or complete.

So, is there an optimal value for the workload metric? The optimum workload metric will be the best trade-off between completing a larger number of projects slowly or a smaller number of projects more quickly. Many resource managers believe it's most efficient to load resources to their full capacity and allow the resources to manage overloads themselves. Since resource loading is dynamic and influenced by variations in project demand, resources will often vacillate between underloading and overloading, never having a chance to reach any kind of smooth workflow.

Let's look at the extremes to determine the range of the workload metric (the minimum and maximum values for a given resource pool). The most extreme underloading occurs with sequential operations, where each resource works on only one task at a time, even if they have sufficient capacity to process multiple tasks simultaneously. In sequential operations, the next task doesn't start until the first task is complete. In contrast, the most extreme overloading occurs with 24/7 operations, where tasks come in continuously, regardless of whether the resource pool is ready to process them.

Let's work through an example. To calculate the minimum workload metric, assume one task waits for service to simulate sequential operations. To calculate the maximum workload metric, assume each resource has 24 tasks at any given time waiting for service, to simulate tasks coming in continuously in 24/7 operations. The resource pool's average project length is 10 tasks, and for simplicity, only one worker is in the resource pool.

The minimum and maximum workload metrics for this resource pool would be:

$$\text{Minimum workload metric} = 10\%$$
$$= 1 \text{ task} \div 1 \text{ resource} \div 10 \text{ tasks} \qquad (7)$$

$$\text{Maximum workload metric} = 240\%$$
$$= 24 \text{ tasks} \div 1 \text{ resource} \div 10 \text{ tasks} \qquad (8)$$

Our goal is to optimize the rate of task completions, or work throughput, while minimizing overloads or underloads. Throughput is a measure of output, not efficiency. So, where's the optimal trade-off point within the workload metric range? The optimal workload metric is about 10 percent into the metric's range, starting from the lower limit of the range.[26] In our example, the range is 230 percent (240 percent − 10 percent). Therefore, 10 percent of 230 percent equals 23 percent. Adding 23 percent to the lower limit of 10 percent equals 33 percent, the optimal workload metric. We now know the optimal workload metric, but what do we do with it?

We will use the optimal workload metric to set a target maximum allowable average task backlog for the resource pool. If the resource pool's task backlog remains less than or equal to the target, you can release more work to the resource pool. However, if the average task backlog exceeds

---

[26]Holt and Clark, "Finding the Sweet Spot in Resource Workload," who ran computer simulations that demonstrated the optimal workload metric.

the target, refrain from releasing more work until the resource pool works down some of the backlog.

Given that the optimal workload metric is 23 percent for this resource pool, the average project duration is 10 days, and there is one resource in the resource pool, we can apply the workload metric formula in reverse to calculate the optimal target, as shown in (9).

$$3.3\text{~}3 \text{ tasks in backlog per resource} = 33\% \\ \text{workload metric} \times 10 \text{ days per project} \times 1 \text{ resource} \quad (9)$$

The resource manager will optimize workflow through the resource pool when the resource pool's average task backlog is less than or equal to three tasks. If the backlog increases beyond three tasks, the resource manager will stop assigning new work until the task backlog decreases to three or fewer tasks. If the resource pool changes, perhaps because people become unavailable, the resource manager should recalculate the workload metric.

You might be surprised that the optimal task backlog is so low at only 33 percent of the workload metric range. But it makes sense, and modern queuing theory explains why.

As more users demand services from a resource, the resource's availability decreases, and users must wait longer for service. Queuing theory states that the waiting time for service equals the resource's utilization in percent divided by one minus the utilization percentage.[27]

We can plot this equation on a line chart (see Figure 9.1), with resource utilization on the horizontal axis and the wait time for service calculation on the vertical axis. The curve rises gradually at lower percentages but begins to increase sharply and at an accelerating rate as it approaches 100 percent, forming a steep convex shape. While it's not exponential, it exhibits exponential-like growth behavior in the upper range. The function is undefined at 100 percent, where it has a vertical asymptote.

---

[27]Alexander Georgescu, "Queueing Theory and Practice," *Computer Science Blog @ HdM Stuttgart*, 2019, accessed June 23, 2025, https://blog.mi.hdm-stuttgart.de /index.php/2019/03/11/queueing-theory-and-practice-or-crash-course-in-queueing/.

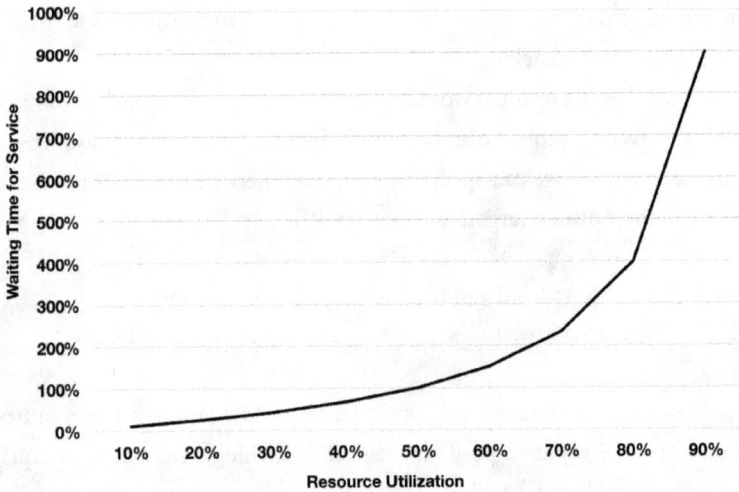

Figure 9.1 Waiting time for service

So, as resource utilization increases, users' wait time for service increases slowly at first, but then at a rapidly accelerating rate.

To interpret the chart, consider 100 percent waiting time for service on the vertical scale as a reference for a normal wait time. Thus, a wait time of 200 percent indicates that users are waiting twice as long as they would at 100 percent.

The curve climbs through 100 percent wait time at only about 50 percent resource utilization. If resource utilization increases to 67 percent, a slight 17 percent absolute increase, wait time *doubles* to 200 percent. If resource utilization increases to 75 percent, wait time *triples* to 300 percent. At 90 percent utilization, wait time increases to 900 percent!

We see this often in action. Resource managers face considerable pressure to achieve 80 to 90 percent resource utilization rates. As shown in Figure 9.1, high utilization leads to user wait times ranging from 400 to 900 percent of the standard 100 percent level. Consequently, workflow through resource pools moves slowly and unpredictably, service quality degrades, and costs and delays escalate. Utilization is excellent, but throughput plummets at an accelerating rate.

The curve in Figure 9.1 also illustrates why the optimal workload metric is toward the lower end of the range. The curve's inflection point is where the slope transitions from rising slowly to rising rapidly, which is between about 50 and 60 percent utilization. If resource utilization is at or below the inflection point, throughput will increase to 100 percent, which is about the best you can do. Above the inflection point, throughput rapidly drops as waiting time for service increases at an accelerating rate. Therefore, average resource pool loading should not exceed 50 to 60 percent utilization, with one possible exception.

Some operations are highly standardized and repetitive, like certain kinds of mass production work. In this case, high utilizations are achievable because the workflow is smooth and easily regulated, as in just-in-time (JIT) manufacturing. But in dynamic, unpredictable workload situations, achieving high resource utilizations should be secondary to achieving high throughput. Unfortunately, most companies measure resource utilization but not throughput, so big drops in output often go undetected until it becomes a crisis.

The workload metric percentage and the resource utilization percentage are often confused. The workload metric percentage measures the average task backlog waiting for resources to become available. Resource utilization measures how much of a resource's capacity is busy and, therefore, unavailable to process additional work. We use the former as an indicator to control when to assign new work to the resource pool to avoid overloads, and the latter to measure the resource pool's efficiency.

Other ways to increase workflow throughput exist. In addition to gating the workflow, management can sequence tasks according to some priority criteria, such as releasing tasks with the earliest start dates, highest profitability, or preferred customer first. You can apply these criteria in conjunction with the workload metric. Management can also provide additional support to resources struggling to complete their assignments. Holt and Clark report that adding business priorities and assisting resources can *double* project throughput beyond gating resource backlog alone.[28]

---

[28]Holt and Clark, "Finding the Sweet Spot in Resource Workload."

Optimizing Resource Usage with a Mathematical Model

Workflow regulation using a workload metric is one of several ways to ensure effective and efficient resource utilization. Another method is to develop a mathematical model that describes how labor hours and equipment usage can meet the demand on a resource pool.[29] The mathematical model is an equation that calculates the time required to provide one service unit, such as the processing time for an order, transaction, delivery, or product. Multiply the processing time per unit by the total demand to calculate the overall processing time. Use the total processing time to determine the staffing and other resources you will need.

Assume a resource manager is responsible for leading an order entry department. The manager must determine the staff required to meet next quarter's projected order entry demand. Assume the resource pool consists of 30 individuals and a standard workweek is 40 hours total, five days per week. According to timing studies, it takes 10 minutes to enter data common to all orders like their names, five minutes to enter each line item ordered, 20 minutes to enter additional data for new customers, and 15 minutes if customers request expediting. A mathematical equation can express these constraints as shown in (10):

$$\text{Process time per order} = 10 \text{ minutes per order} + \\ (5 \text{ minutes} \times \text{number of line items}) + 20 \times \\ [\text{if new customer}] + 15 \times [\text{if expedited order}] \tag{10}$$

The terms in brackets are conditional. You should read them as "If this condition is true, add the coefficient before the brackets. Otherwise, add zero." The equation includes conditional expressions to model all possibilities to process an order. For example, if a typical order for a new customer includes three line items and doesn't require

[29]Robert S. Kaplan, and Steven R. Anderson. "Time-Driven Activity-Based Costing," *Harvard Business Review* 82, no. 11 (2004): 131–38, accessed June 23, 2025. https://hbr.org/2004/11/time-driven-activity-based-costing.

expediting, the average processing time per order is 45 minutes, as shown in (11):

$$45 \text{ minutes avg processing time per order}$$
$$= 10 \text{ minutes per standard order}$$
$$+ (5 \text{ minutes per line item} \times 3 \text{ line items}) \qquad (11)$$
$$+ 20 \text{ minutes for a new customer}$$
$$+ (15 \text{ minutes for expedited requests} \times 0 \text{ requests})$$

This 45-minute average processing time is for one combination of conditions. To calculate the average processing time across all possible combinations of conditions, we need data on the percentages of orders for new customers and expedited processing requests, and the average number of line items per order. The data is usually available from a company's orders database, and if not, employees can often provide rough estimates.

To see how calculating resource demand works, let's work through an example. Assume the following:

1. Ten minutes of standard processing per order.
2. Five minutes to process each line item.
3. An average of five line items per order.
4. Twenty minutes to process a new customer.
5. Twenty-five percent of orders are for new customers.
6. Fifteen minutes to process expedited orders.
7. Fifteen percent of customers request expediting of their orders.
8. All current order entry staff are fully loaded.
9. Next quarter's sales forecast increases by 5,000 orders.
10. Employees take three weeks of paid vacation annually.

The calculations are shown step by step in (12) through (16). The result in (16) means that over seven additional people must be hired to support the forecasted increase in demand next quarter. The decimal portion implies the resource manager can hire seven FTE and be slightly understaffed, or hire eight FTE and have 0.8 FTE of reserve labor capacity.

$$42.25 \text{ minutes per order} = 10 \text{ minutes per standard order} + \\ (5 \text{ minutes per line item} \times 5 \text{ line items}) + (20 \text{ minutes} \\ \text{for a new customer} \times 0.25 \text{ percent new customers}) + \\ (15 \text{ minutes per expedited order} \times 0.15 \text{ percent expedited}) \tag{12}$$

$$211{,}250 \text{ minutes per quarter} = 42.25 \text{ minutes} \\ \text{per order} \times 5{,}000 \text{ orders} \tag{13}$$

$$440.1 \text{ workdays} = 211{,}250 \text{ minutes} \div 60 \text{ minutes} \\ \text{per hour} \div 8 \text{ hours per workday} \tag{14}$$

$$61.25 \text{ workdays per quarter} = 49 \text{ weeks} \times \\ 5 \text{ workdays per week} \div 4 \text{ quarters per year} \tag{15}$$

$$7.2 \text{ FTE} = 440.1 \text{ workdays} \div 61.25 \text{ workdays} \\ \text{per person per quarter} \tag{16}$$

The same model can also calculate the average cost per order. The goal is to drive down processing time and cost per order, provided the quality of the work is maintained or improved. As noted previously, next quarter's demand forecast increases by 5,000 orders. The total processing time for these additional 5,000 orders is 211,250 minutes, as calculated in (12) and (13). Assume it costs $550,000 per quarter to run the department, including costs of employees, office space, phones, computers, and other expenses.

The equation to calculate total cost per minute is in (17). Since the average processing time per order is 42.25 minutes, as shown in (12), the total cost per order is in (18):

$$\$2.60 \text{ per minute} = \$550{,}000 \div 211{,}250 \text{ minutes} \tag{17}$$

$$\$109.85 \text{ per order} = \$2.60 \text{ per minute} \times \\ 42.25 \text{ minutes per order} \tag{18}$$

The workload metric from the previous section and the mathematical model are not mutually exclusive. The workload metric helps manage resource allocation decisions in real time. The mathematical model applies to planning capacity, staffing, and transaction costs.

As a Senior Vice President, a business management function once reported to me. The business owners questioned why the function had more headcount than similar functions in other divisions. I trained the business manager to develop a mathematical model of her function. She kept logs for a month to identify sources of demand, processing times, and contingent demands. Once she had the data, I helped her construct the model. The data showed that our project portfolio was significantly more complex and extensive than that of the other divisions, resulting in a substantially higher demand for business management services. The higher demand was consistent with our business model design. We all agreed that the business management group had the correct headcount.

Summary

Many resource managers struggle to manage resource capacity across demand, resulting in schedule and cost overruns. Queuing theory indicates that resource utilization should not exceed 60 percent, since resource productivity significantly decreases and user wait times for service dramatically increase beyond that threshold. Most companies strive for 80 to 90 percent utilization on all resources to avoid wasting resource capacity, but all they end up doing is decimating throughput, and all projects fall behind.

Another solution is to use a workload metric to control the flow of work into the resource pool. The idea is to hold incoming tasks until each resource's backlog decreases to the metric's target threshold, after which you can then release more work to the resource. Your goal is to calculate the workload metric's target to optimize the trade-off between capacity underutilization, meaning not processing tasks when resources are available, and capacity overallocation, when no resources are available because they're all busy. You can also calculate a mathematical model, an equation, that optimizes resource capacity for a projected level of demand.

While this sounds complex, it's straightforward with simple math as described in this chapter.

Finally, organizing product development projects matters. You should use core teams composed of standardized roles and project-based organizations to align authority with responsibility and accountability.

At this point, we've covered market, design, and development blind spots and how to prevent or mitigate their impacts on new product market failures and overruns. But we haven't yet discussed common blind spots that affect sales growth and profitability post-launch, which is the subject of the following chapters in Part III.

Reader Call to Action

How you manage resource allocation and capacity is critical to effective project execution. Your challenge is to consider how to execute product development based on insights from previous Reader Calls to Action. Here are key questions to ask yourself:

1. How will you structure your project team?
    a. Will you use the standard core roles?
    b. Who will fill the roles?
    c. Will you use the Who/What/How conflict resolution model to manage conflicts?
2. What functional organizations will support your project and provide it with resources?
    a. Will these resources be multitasked?
        i. If so, what percentage of their capacity will be devoted to your project?
        ii. If your baseline schedule assumes full staffing, how will you manage the schedule and cost impacts?
3. Do resource managers providing resources to your project use metrics or mathematical models to ensure they stay on schedule?

Lessons Learned

1. Use project-based organizations to execute product development projects, which ensures authority, responsibility, and accountability. Use functional organizations to develop inputs like expertise, infrastructure, processes, or capabilities.

2. Establish core teams with standardized leadership roles to execute projects effectively. The most common roles are the PM, TM, MM, QM, and SCM.

3. These roles lead the project, technical design, manufacturing, quality, and supplier activities. Senior people with the appropriate experience, expertise, and training should fill the roles.

4. Manage resource capacity to avoid overruns. Three techniques to do this include:

   a. Use a quantitative workload metric to indicate when to release more work to the resource pool without creating an overload.

   b. Limit resource utilization to no more than 50 to 60 percent, as exceeding this threshold results in a significant drop in resource productivity and a substantial increase in user waiting times for service.

   c. Develop a mathematical equation to manage resource capacity against demand.

PART III

Drive Sales and Profitability

Ideally, you've developed your new product without overruns, and it delivers what customers want. However, after launch, many companies struggle with three critical challenges: forecasting demand, managing sales campaigns, and pricing for profitability. These are often subject to unjustified optimism, yet another blind spot in product development. This part explores common challenges companies face when launching new products and guides how to overcome them.

CHAPTER 10

Plan Order Forecasts and Sales Campaigns

By now, you've successfully identified customer needs, developed new products, and launched them into the market. However, there are still challenges ahead. A golden opportunity exists to delay or slow down the market ramp.

Each customer experiences a journey from initial awareness of the company's product through final delivery and use. This journey has multiple segments, with dropouts at each stage. Dropouts occur when customers decide not to buy. A customer's journey is like a funnel, with many sales opportunities entering at the top and fewer orders flowing out at the bottom.

Most companies track the progress of orders through the sales funnel to generate sales forecasts and revenue plans needed by the board of directors, executives, investors, and lenders. However, they can get into serious trouble when their sales forecasts are inaccurate, which happens frequently. Many companies define a sales forecasting algorithm, but they often don't consider its accuracy. Failing to track sales forecasting accuracy is a significant organizational blind spot, as companies must manage their sales forecasts, make accurate revenue commitments, and achieve them through effective sales campaigns.

Modeling Sales Opportunities with a Funnel Metaphor

Most companies refer to the sales funnel as the sales pipeline. However, a pipeline is a poor metaphor because the order flow in most companies is much more volatile than the smooth flow of water through a pipe. Orders drop out at each stage of the buying process, and some loop back to an earlier stage. This false assumption of smooth order flow deceives companies into believing their sales forecasts are more predictable than what typically occurs. As a result, companies falsely assume that mathematical expected values can accurately estimate sales forecasts. Let's examine this in more detail.

An expected value is a weighted average of each order's dollar amount times its probability of occurrence. For example, if two orders are worth $1 million each, and their probabilities of winning (P-Win) are 80 percent and 60 percent, respectively, the expected value would be:

$$\$1.4 \text{ million} = \$800,000 \ (80\% \text{ of } \$1 \text{ million}) \\ + \$600,000 \ (60\% \text{ of } \$1 \text{ million}) \tag{19}$$

The problem with this forecast is that it's virtually guaranteed to be wrong. The expected value will only happen with a statistically large number of forecasts because it's a weighted average. The actual outcome for any of the two orders will be zero (no wins), $1 million (either order wins), or $2 million (both orders win). So, if the expected value is used for the sales forecast, the variance will be –$1.4 million, –$400,000, or $600,000, respectively. The negative variances are unfavorable and result in undershooting the revenue forecast, while the one positive (favorable) variance results in overshooting.

Another problem is that the probability estimate may be highly subjective, with no statistical justification, which makes the probability a guess or, worse, a biased forecast subject to unjustified optimism.

Some companies recognize these issues and use a different system that assigns a fixed probability, like 80 percent, to any order forecast they expect or intend to win. They track all lower-probability forecasts but exclude them from the sales forecast. The only benefit of this approach is that the probability is applied consistently, but the forecaster still must decide which sales opportunities are above or below the line. However, the forecast is still a weighted average. The binary nature of an order, win or lose, ensures the forecast will still be wrong most of the time.

A more accurate sales forecasting method estimates sales forecasts using sales funnel dropout rates. Since all orders in the sales funnel affect the dropout rates, the aggregated data improve accuracy as the organization grows and gains more sales experience.

Companies often define different names for sales funnel stages, but there are typically five common stages:

1. Leads
2. Sales calls
3. Quotes
4. Conversions
5. Orders

Sales opportunities may drop out at any stage when customers decide not to buy for any reason. In the leads stage, the salesperson identifies initial, unqualified sales opportunities. Unqualified means the company doesn't know yet if a customer has money and is ready to buy.

The second stage, sales calls, involves salespeople engaging with customers to determine whether they can afford the product and are ready to buy. Salespeople also educate customers about product options, applications, and configurations best suited to their needs.

The third stage, quotes, involves salespeople providing customers with pricing and delivery information, and answering any questions they may have. Companies with simple products or who sell through third parties may skip this step.

In the fourth stage, conversion, customers make buying decisions, including engaging in technical, pricing, and contract negotiations.

In the final and fifth stage, orders, customers place orders or execute purchase agreements.

Dropout rates are critical and proprietary data because they measure order losses at each stage of the sales funnel. Instead of only a binary estimate for each order (won or lost), dropout rates provide information on where in the funnel, and how often, order losses occur. The location of order dropouts in the sales funnel can help explain why the company loses business.

Estimating Order Forecasts Using Sales Funnel Dropout Rates

A dropout rate is the ratio of sales opportunities in an upstream stage of the sales funnel to sales opportunities in a downstream stage. For example, if 125 leads result in one order, the ratio of leads to orders is 125 to one. If half of all leads result in sales calls, the ratio of leads to sales calls is two to one. As the dataset grows, dropout rates stabilize because larger sample sizes average out outliers.

Dropout rates help estimate how many orders will exit from the bottom of the sales funnel based on a specific number of leads entering at the top. For example, if the funnel dropout ratio from leads to orders is 125 to one, and 1,000 leads are in process, we can expect to secure eight orders (1,000 divided by 125). If the average order size is $1 million, eight orders would generate $8 million in sales.

By tracking the cycle time for each sales funnel stage, we can determine when sales should occur and forecast accordingly. For example, assume the average cycle time from initial lead to the final order is three months. Also, assume that we are planning for third-quarter sales targets. Since the cycle time is three months, plan market promotion and lead generating activities to start at the beginning of the second quarter.

Using the Sales Funnel to Plan Sales Campaigns

Assume the company wins 18 orders for every 50 leads, or 0.36 orders per lead. See Figure 10.1.

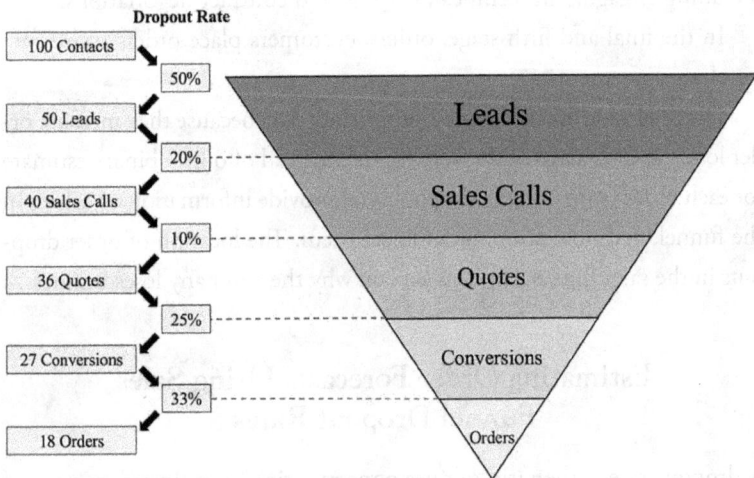

Figure 10.1 Sales funnel with dropout rates

If the order target is $20 million and the average order size is $500,000, the company must win at least 40 orders and generate 111 leads, as shown in (20) and (21):

$$\begin{array}{c} \$20 \text{ million orders target} \div \$500,000 \\ \text{average order size} = 40 \text{ orders} \end{array} \quad (20)$$

$$111 \text{ leads} = 40 \text{ orders} \div 0.36 \text{ orders per lead} \quad (21)$$

The marketing and sales budget must be high enough to generate at least 111 leads to achieve the order target. Similar calculations can be made for the other sales funnel stages, as shown in (22) through (27). To achieve 18 orders, the sales force must make 89 sales calls as shown in (22) and (23), 80 quotes in (24) and (25), and 60 conversions in (26) and (27):

$$0.45 \text{ orders per sales call} = 18 \text{ orders} \div 40 \text{ sales calls} \quad (22)$$

$$89 \text{ sales calls} = 40 \text{ orders} \div 0.45 \text{ orders per sales call} \quad (23)$$

$$0.50 \text{ orders per quotes} = 18 \text{ orders} \div 36 \text{ quotes} \quad (24)$$

$$80 \text{ quotes} = 40 \text{ orders} \div 0.50 \text{ orders per quote} \quad (25)$$

$$0.67 \text{ orders per conversion} = 18 \text{ orders} \div 27 \text{ conversions} \quad (26)$$

$$60 \text{ conversions} = 40 \text{ orders} + 0.67 \text{ orders per conversion} \quad (27)$$

If the company tracks the cost of each stage, it can use the results of (20) through (27) to calculate unit costs such as cost per lead, cost per sales call, and so on. You can compare estimated unit costs to industry benchmarks to develop performance targets and determine if the company's cost structure is competitive and efficient.

Some companies, particularly in aerospace and defense, may compete for a small number of very large contract opportunities. For example, when I was a senior executive, one of the product lines in my organization designed, developed, and produced small satellites for the U.S. government.

These were multimillion-dollar satellites with national security payloads. One contract would last at least a few years or more and involve building multiple satellites for a constellation of satellites. The number of contract opportunities in a year was perhaps a handful or two at best, so these fit in the small-number-of-significant-opportunities category.

The problem with this kind of business is that short-term dropout rates are too coarse to generate sales forecasts. As part of our operating plan, we forecasted only those specific opportunities for which we could commit resources to win. We tracked all other opportunities in the sales funnel but excluded them from the sales forecast. At the other end of the spectrum, I worked in a cardiac pacemaker company that produced thousands of units monthly in a highly competitive market. The large number of unit sales generated enough data to assess dropout rates at each stage of the sales process.

Tracking Sales Opportunities Moving Through the Funnel

Most companies track sales opportunities as they move through the sales funnel, typically with Customer Relationship Management (CRM) software tools such as Salesforce, Microsoft Dynamics 365, and HubSpot. However, there are many more. These tools capture vital sales and customer data, including contact information, products ordered, shipment status, order history, and sales funnel stage, among many other data elements. A well-designed CRM system will capture red flags, such as the risk of losing an order, business-to-business buyer roles, and sales actions. A less common but valuable use of a CRM tool is to calculate and track sales funnel dropout rates.

In the next and final chapter, we'll discuss common blind spots in project finance, product costing, and pricing and what to do about them.

Summary

Sales forecasts, cost estimates, and market pricing are subject to blind spots similar to those found in earlier stages of product development. These blind spots lead to optimistic sales forecasts in terms of timing and magnitude, resulting in missed revenue growth targets and commitments. Optimistic cost estimates result in unplanned, higher costs and lower profitability. Market pricing often decreases more rapidly than anticipated, primarily due to intense competition. Companies need tools to predict and manage the effects of these blind spots, ensuring successful sales growth.

Many companies use a pipeline metaphor to describe the journey every customer takes through the sales process, from initial awareness to final delivery and use of the product or service. However, a pipeline metaphor imagines a constant, smooth flow, which is not how sales processes work. Customers drop out at every stage of the sales process when they decide not to buy and leave the buying process. Common reasons for not buying may include affordability, purchasing from a competitor, opting for a different solution, doing it themselves, or simply not buying at all.

The dropout rates at each stage help make sales and profitability forecasts more realistic, enabling more accurate planning of resource allocations for sales campaigns. Over time, as data accumulates, the dropout rates and sales forecasts will become more accurate.

Many companies use mathematical expected values to forecast sales, which is inaccurate unless statistically valid data are available. Using expected values for sales forecasting is a blind spot that results in missed sales growth targets, so a better alternative is to use the sales funnel's dropout rates model instead. You can also use the sales funnel's dropout rates in reverse to plan sales campaigns. Since dropout rates occur for every stage of the sales process, you can back-calculate how many initial leads, sales calls, and other activities are required to generate a target number of orders to achieve revenue forecasts.

The next and final chapter examines blind spots in cost estimating, which frequently lead to overly optimistic cost estimates and poor profitability.

Reader Call to Action

Imagine that your new product development project is complete, and the product is ready to launch. How will you forecast sales and make revenue commitments to key stakeholders? Will you use mathematical expected values, a percentage of the market, commitments to secure specific orders, estimated sales funnel dropout rates, or a combination of these approaches to make your forecasts?

If you have low-volume, high-dollar-value opportunities, forecast sales by committing to winning specific orders and planning for what happens if you lose them.

Otherwise, research to estimate sales funnel dropout rates and use them to forecast how many orders you need to secure to meet your revenue target. You can also estimate how many leads, sales calls, demonstrations, and conversions are necessary to generate your target number of orders. Base your research on discussions with industry experts, your own experience, your team's experience, and published sources. After making initial forecasts and commitments, you can update your dropout rates as you gather more market data.

Lessons Learned

1. Companies forecast sales to plan growth and manage their businesses. The most common method is calculating subjective expected values, which are probability-weighted averages of multiple forecasts. However, most companies lack statistical data to back up their expected value sales forecasts, which makes them inaccurate.

2. Unjustified optimism is the largest source of inaccurate sales forecasts because companies typically set aggressive sales targets to drive growth. Still, they underestimate how much competition and market changes reduce sales. Orders tend to be later and smaller than forecast, resulting in missed sales targets and potential financial losses.

3. A more effective approach to forecasting sales involves utilizing dropout rates from the sales funnel. A dropout rate is the percentage of orders that drop out of the sales funnel at a given point in the customer's journey from awareness to placing an order.

4. Startups and companies with low volume and large contracts may need to use a different system where they list their sales opportunities and decide which ones they'll commit to winning. The winning opportunities go into the sales forecast, and all others remain in the sales funnel.

5. The sales funnel model can be applied in reverse to plan sales campaign activities. Once dropout rates are known, you can easily calculate how many activities are needed to achieve the sales forecasts.

CHAPTER 11

Drive Profitability After Market Launch

We've covered schedule overruns in depth, so now it's time to discuss managing profitability after market launch, mostly by how to estimate costs to determine accurate pricing. We will examine typical cost-estimating blind spots and what to do about them. However, let's first discuss basic concepts of project finance, pricing, and bottom-up cost estimating.

Cost estimating should be straightforward because the costs of materials and labor rates are generally well known. However, many costs are dynamic, which makes them difficult to estimate in advance. For example, most companies budget for indirect costs at the beginning of a fiscal year. These costs are allocated to all projects as they incur labor and material expenses. Actual indirect costs are rarely the same as budgeted costs since projects and organizations are dynamic, leading to changes that may cause cost overruns. The project team has no control over rate changes but is often held responsible for adverse cost impacts.

Defining Direct and Indirect Costs

Direct costs are proportional to production volume. For example, building each product or delivering each service generates labor costs. Indirect costs are constant, which means indirect spending occurs regardless of changes in production volume. Indirect costs include office space, lighting, facilities, supervision, tools, marketing, finance, HR, and IT, among many others. Direct costs are also called variable costs, and indirect costs are called fixed costs. The variable and fixed terminology is used mainly in profitability calculations, while contract management, indirect rates management, and cost allocation discussions tend to use direct and indirect terminology. In this book, we'll stick with direct and indirect terminology.

To survive over the long term, a company must charge a price per unit of at least the total costs per unit plus a reasonable profit. Total costs are equal to the sum of total direct costs plus total indirect costs. Determining total direct costs is straightforward because they're directly associated with each unit built or service delivered. But how should indirect costs be identified since they're not associated with a particular product?

One solution is to allocate indirect costs to each unit of product or service. To allocate means to prorate a pooled budget according to some base value. For example, overhead typically includes all indirect costs of supporting production, such as facilities, lighting, equipment, tooling, and production supervision. Overhead supports production, so allocating it over the total number of units produced makes sense. Total costs to build one unit equal total direct costs plus allocated overhead costs. Other indirect costs are allocated similarly but against a different base pool. For example, materials handling indirect expenses, which include costs of storing, tracking, moving, and securing direct materials, are typically allocated across total direct materials costs.

If production volume is low, such as with products or services limited to a small customer base requiring customization, high-end luxury, high complexity, or high quality, using the product as the base wouldn't make sense. Such products might be limited-edition consumer electronics, custom medical devices like prosthetics and surgical tools, luxury car customizations, or spacecraft. In this case, the base for overhead is usually direct labor charged to the contract. The base for materials handling would be direct materials charged to the contract.

Other indirect pooled budgets besides overhead and materials handling often exist. For example, General & Administrative (G&A) costs include all indirect, enterprise-wide business costs such as the CEO's salary, IT, HR, security, finance, and marketing. Another indirect pool covers supplier subcontract handling costs, including the cost of subcontract managers. Companies often combine subcontract and materials handling costs and allocate them across total subcontract and materials costs. The combined indirect rate is called the MAT/SUB rate.

Sometimes, companies combine MAT/SUB costs under overhead or all indirect costs under overhead. The Chief Financial Officer (CFO) or equivalent usually decides the indirect cost structure. The government publishes detailed guidance to contractors on developing indirect rate structures, which is also helpful for private sector companies.[30]

Companies allocate overhead costs based on direct labor dollars spent to produce products and services. The ratio of total overhead costs to direct labor is called the overhead rate. Companies allocate G&A costs based on total enterprise costs because G&A supports the entire company. Total enterprise costs typically include all direct labor, fringe benefits, overhead, travel, materials, subcontracts, and Other Direct Costs (ODC) like consulting services, travel, or printing. Companies allocate MAT/SUB handling costs based on direct materials and subcontract management costs.

Let's review how to calculate an indirect rate. Assume a company's total G&A costs are $1.5 million and total enterprise costs (the G&A base) are $10 million. The company's G&A Rate is 15 percent and shown in (28):

$$\text{\$1.5 million G\&A} \div \text{\$10 million G\&A base} = 0.15 = 15\% \quad (28)$$

Now that we know the G&A rate, we can calculate how much G&A expense to allocate to a given product. If the total cost to produce 1,000 units is $1 million, then the allocated G&A expense for each unit of product is calculated in (29):

$$(0.15 \times \text{\$1 million}) \div 1{,}000 \text{ units} = \text{\$150 per unit} \quad (29)$$

If direct costs are $200 per unit, total costs are $200 + $150 = $350 per unit. Profit is added to total costs to calculate the customer's price.

---

[30]U.S. Department of Labor, *A Guide for Indirect Cost Rate Determination* (Cost & Price Determination Division, Office of Strategy & Administration/OSPE /OASAM, 2024), https://www.dol.gov/sites/dolgov/files/OASAM/legacy/files /DCD-2-CFR-Guide.pdf. Some government websites are blocked for international access. Contact the author at info@targemetrics.com for a copy of the source.

Leveraging Contribution Margins to Grow Revenue

Indirect cost allocations ensure a company recovers indirect costs through sales. People often refer to this fully allocated cost more generally as the product's cost. The common assumption is that the company will lose money if competition forces a product's price below cost. However, this isn't always true because a company may decide not to include indirect cost allocations in the unit price.

Over the long term, a company must sell its products above the total, fully allocated cost. The difference between the total cost and the price is profit. However, suppose the company's price is too high, and the product isn't selling well. Because of reduced shipments, the company's manufacturing plant has substantial unused capacity. The company urgently needs to drive sales, but it's also worried that further price cuts will drive the unit price below cost, causing a loss for each unit sold. They must find a solution.

Remember, total cost includes direct costs and allocated indirect costs. Indirect costs don't change with changes in production volume. The company will incur indirect costs regardless of whether it changes the price. Therefore, indirect costs are irrelevant to this decision, at least in the short term.

Suppose a competitive price is less than total costs but above direct costs. If the company reduces the price to compete, the difference between the new price and direct costs *contributes* to partially recovering indirect costs, hence the name, contribution margin.

The increased sales help maintain market share and give the company more time to find a long-term solution, such as redesigning the product to reduce costs or outsourcing manufacturing. Reducing prices below total costs is not sustainable in the long term because the company does not fully recover indirect costs.

I once consulted for a large company with much spare capacity. Sales were low because the finance department set the product's unit price well above the market to recover the indirect costs of past technology investments. The sales department reacted to the low sales rate by reducing sales forecasts. Lower sales forecasts forced a lower assumed future direct base. A lower direct base necessitated a higher allocation to cover past investment costs, resulting in a higher sales price. The situation was a race to the bottom.

Not surprisingly, the company missed its operating plan targets. The marketing and sales functions wanted to cut the price to be competitive, while the finance function insisted on allocating all fixed costs. Neither party would change its position.

I explained how contribution margins work and proposed that the company reduce the unit price to a competitive level while maintaining a positive contribution margin. The finance function would not accept a price reduction less than the fully allocated price because it would cause a loss on paper, even though it made sense economically. After all, the contribution margin was positive, and spare capacity was available. Marketing refused to raise its sales forecasts without a price cut. Both sides stuck to their position, and sales continued to decline. Eventually, the company wrote off the entire investment.

Matching Indirect Rates to Your Business Model

Another common project finance mistake is when a company chooses an indirect rate structure that doesn't match its business model, often resulting in uncompetitive indirect rates that drive up contract and product prices.

A company's indirect rate structure reflects how efficiently management operates enterprise-wide administrative and support functions like accounting, finance, marketing, sales, executive staff, HR, facilities, production support, and IT. Comparing rate structures is an excellent way to evaluate how efficiently companies within an industry manage their businesses. The U.S. government knows this, so it reviews and approves indirect rates for government contractors to ensure it does not overpay for products and services. The government also wants to ensure suppliers recover their fixed costs so they will survive in the long term. A stable supply chain is critical for the government because it often procures unique, long-lasting products like national defense systems.

Some companies are susceptible to indirect rate fluctuations, especially integrators refurbishing or upgrading complex systems like aircraft. These kinds of businesses require a sizable direct labor base, which generates a lot of overhead and G&A through the rates. The OH and G&A rates include direct labor in their base (the denominators). If the base increases, the numerators increase by a corresponding amount to maintain the rates.

It's possible to grow these companies through investments financed by the rates. Because the government reimburses suppliers for indirect costs budgeted in the rates, indirect budget increases paid for by the government are effectively a financing source. Rates-based financing is desirable for owners of government contractors who wish to retain control of their businesses without raising money from outside investors.

A business that designs and develops custom products, such as artwork, home additions, unique fine furniture, aircraft, or spacecraft, has a different business model than an integration-based business that upgrades other manufacturers' products, such as converting standard vans into luxury recreational vehicles.

Increased design and manufacturing activities, along with a greater reliance on the supply chain, primarily drive the design-based business. It's common for design-intensive firms to outsource 60 to 70 percent of a project's value to outside vendors. This results in a smaller direct labor base than an integration-based business, which buys a stock vehicle and some materials and spends labor to rebuild and upgrade it. Lower direct labor generates upward pressure on the rates because the base is smaller. The design-based business spends more on capital equipment and Internal Research and Development (IR&D) to support manufacturing and new product development, which also causes upward pressure on the rates. Generally, a design-intensive business will be a net consumer of investment. Its rates should be higher to compensate.

An integration-based business will be a net generator of investment because it doesn't design and build the product from scratch. Direct labor is higher, but overhead and support costs should be lower. Combining a higher base with lower indirect costs should result in lower rates.

If an integrator has high rates and a product manufacturer has low rates, both will be in trouble. The integrator will incur higher indirect costs and must charge higher prices accordingly, which can make it uncompetitive. The product manufacturer will need more investment, which limits growth unless the business can raise funding from outside investors. If your product is uncompetitive, look hard at your indirect rates model. Your support functions may be inefficient and expensive.

Multidivisional and privately owned companies often maintain one set of indirect rates for the entire enterprise, simplifying rates management and supporting centralized investment decisions. Integration-based business units with a high base can subsidize design-based business units with a low base. Cross-subsidies may be an efficient way for a government contractor to allocate investment budgets funded by the rates. However, from the government's or an investor's perspective, cross-subsidies are a worst-of-all-worlds scenario.

Since integration-based businesses have a higher base and require less investment, they should have lower indirect budgets to reduce their indirect rates. Lower rates generate lower indirect costs, allowing lower prices and producing more revenue growth. In contrast, design-intensive companies require more investment and larger supply chains, so they should have higher indirect budgets, which increases their rates. As a result, your goal should be to optimize indirect rates for each business unit without cross-subsidies, which ensures competitive pricing and efficient management of each business.

Justify All Cost Estimates with a Basis of Estimate

Bottom-up price calculations start from direct costs and then add indirect costs and fees to arrive at a total price. We need to know the project work scope before starting bottom-up price calculations. Work scope is the work on a project expressed as a time-phased plan.

A Basis of Estimate (BOE) is a written description of the rationale for a cost estimate and may include calculations, methods, data, logic, and assumptions used to estimate costs. The U.S. Government Accountability Office (GAO) publishes a free guide for cost estimating aptly called the *Cost Estimating and Assessment Guide.*[31] Unless a company is a government contractor, it doesn't have to comply with the government's guidance. However, the guide is a great place to start to learn cost estimating.

---

[31]U.S. GAO (Government Accountability Office), *Cost Estimating and Assessment Guide: Best Practices for Developing and Managing Program Costs,* GAO-20-195G, 2020, https://www.gao.gov/assets/gao-20-195g.pdf. Some government websites are blocked for international access. Contact the author at info@targemetrics. com for a copy of the source.

The most common problem is that many estimators use overly simplified spreadsheets to determine the work scope because they don't know how to use project management scheduling software. The problem with spreadsheets is that they are static tables with data and formulas. That's not how projects work. Projects are dynamic because upstream delays become the starting point for downstream activities. As a result, delays ripple through the task network, which may require many schedule calculations if the task network is complex. It's best to use a software scheduling engine designed to make these calculations.

Microsoft Project is popular in the aerospace and defense industries because it provides detailed resource management, Gantt charts, timesheet integration, and strong reporting features. Oracle Primavera specializes in construction and other heavy industries. JIRA specializes in software development. There are many project management applications, so the key is to ensure they capture a project network, compute the schedule, identify the critical path, roll up costs, and provide the reporting you need. You can check online for comparative analyses and recommendations for project management software at Techradar and Gartner Group, or do a keyword search on project management software through an AI tool like ChatGPT or Google.[32]

Cost estimating for large projects quickly becomes laborious and complex due to the numerous activities involved. To reduce complexity, cost estimators estimate costs at a summary level. Estimating with summary tasks is often another source of cost overrun risk because they are typically simplified, frequently making them optimistic.

Write a BOE for each cost estimate to explain its rationale. Many companies skip this step entirely, and they pay dearly for it. Without documented BOEs, it's difficult for reviewers to assess the accuracy of the estimates. In addition, the lack of BOEs forces each bid or proposal to start from scratch. Most companies lack a central repository to store work scope, schedules, and cost information for past projects, which hinders efforts to improve estimating accuracy. Bid teams don't learn from each other, which perpetuates estimating errors. Most executives don't even

---

[32]Jonas P. DeMuro, "Best Project Management Software," *Techradar*, 2025, accessed June 23, 2025, https://www.techradar.com/best/best-project-management-software.

recognize how the lack of a BOE repository causes future overruns, so most of the time, nothing changes.

Another common mistake in cost estimating is not using RCF as a reality check. The idea is to validate cost estimates against the experiences of others with projects of similar size, complexity, and required innovation. If your estimates are half the budget of what other companies spent, what makes your team so much better?

Finally, watch for the planning fallacy. It's always hiding in the background, inherent in human nature. People tend estimate optimistically, regardless of their efforts to be conservative. Optimistic estimates lead to overruns. RCF is the best solution to prevent unjustified optimism. Still, few companies use it because it's easier and faster to generate estimates bottom-up, even if they're less accurate.

Calculating Bottom-Up Estimates for Pricing Decisions

A bottom-up pricing estimate begins with direct labor, defined as labor to build one product, deliver one service, or execute a contract. Most companies categorize labor using standardized job titles and descriptions. Each labor category has an assigned labor rate in dollars per hour. Many labor categories are hierarchical based on increasing seniority, experience, and responsibilities, with higher labor rates in the upper levels of the hierarchy.

Cost estimators usually don't know which labor categories will do the work in the future, so they typically make assumptions. Basing cost estimates on future events creates a risk of overruns because resource availability and project workloads are highly dynamic. Therefore, labor hour estimates are the first place to look if cost overruns happen.

Like any forecast, labor hour estimates are often optimistic, causing direct labor costs to be higher than planned. However, even if the labor hours estimate is correct, the assumed labor rate may be wrong. For example, the cost estimator may believe that an entry-level engineer will work on a task, but later, the resource manager assigns a senior engineer. While a senior engineer should be able to complete the work in fewer hours, the higher labor rate may more than offset the labor hour reduction. So, two variables are at play with direct labor: assumed labor hours and assumed labor rate. Both can be sources of cost overruns. See Table 11.1 for an example of a direct labor cost estimate.

Table 11.1 Direct labor

Top-level Labor categories	Labor hours	Labor rate ($/hour)	Total
Design Engineering	13,333	$75.00	$1,000,000
Operations Engineering	7,857	$70.00	$550,000
Production	60,000	$50.00	$3,000,000
Total Direct Labor	81,190		$4,550,000

Fringe Costs

Employees receive fringe benefits such as health care, paid time off, employee assistance programs, and sick time. The company must allocate fringe costs to the contract or product price in two steps to recover them. The first step is calculating the fringe rate by dividing total fringe costs by total direct labor. The fringe rate is typically around 30 to 40 percent, but it varies by industry. The CFO usually calculates and approves all indirect rates in advance, including the fringe rate. Assume the fringe rate is 37 percent. See fringe costs calculations in (30).

$4.55 million direct labor × 37% fringe rate = $1,683,500   (30)

See Table 11.2 for fringe costs added to the model.

Table 11.2 Fringe

Top-level labor categories	Indirect rate	Labor hours	Labor rate ($/hour)	Total
Design Engineering		13,333	$75.00	$1,000,000
Operations Engineering		7,857	$70.00	$550,000
Production		60,000	$50.00	$3,000,000
Total Direct Labor		81,190		$4,550,000
Total Fringe	37%			$1,683,500

Indirect cost allocations are another source of error in pricing calculations. The company calculates the rates at the beginning of the fiscal year based on indirect and direct budgeted costs. Like any prediction, the company makes assumptions about future staffing and contract awards. These assumptions are often incorrect due to uncertainties. Direct labor costs will be lower than assumed if orders fall behind the plan, and indirect costs will be higher because actions to reduce indirect costs tend to lag order shortfalls (it takes time for most companies to react). As a result, rates may increase, so indirect costs allocated to the project will be higher than the original cost estimates using budgeted rates. Because multiple indirect cost allocations often exist, these errors tend to multiply.

Overhead

The next step is to add overhead costs. Overhead (OH) is the cost of support to production and includes budgets for depreciation expense, production space, lease costs, training, and production management. The company calculates the OH rate by dividing the total OH by the total direct labor. To determine the OH allocation, multiply the project's total direct labor by the OH rate. Assume an OH rate of 95 percent. See OH calculations in (31).

$$\$4.55 \text{ million direct labor} \times 95\% \text{ OH rate}$$
$$= \$4,322,500 \text{ total OH} \tag{31}$$

Some companies establish multiple overhead rates when support costs vary significantly across different functions. For instance, if production and engineering use separate facilities, a company may create separate overhead rates for each of them. Both overhead and direct labor costs are variable, so cost estimates will likely diverge from actual expenditures, presenting another risk. See Table 11.3 for overhead costs.

Table 11.3 Overhead

Top-level labor categories	Indirect rate (%)	Labor hours	Labor rate ($/hour)	Total
Design Engineering		13,333	$75.00	$1,000,000
Operations Engineering		7,857	$70.00	$550,000
Production		<u>60,000</u>	$50.00	<u>$3,000,000</u>
Total Direct Labor		**81,190**		**$4,550,000**
Total Fringe	37			$1,683,500
Total Overhead	95			$4,322,500

Materials and Subcontracts

The next step is to allocate Materials and Subcontract (MAT/SUB) costs, which are calculated based on a materials handling and subcontract management rate. Some companies split materials and subcontracts into separate rates if each is large enough. Others merge them into OH. Assume $15 million for MAT/SUB costs. These costs serve as the base for the MAT/SUB handling rate, which is typically around 8 percent. See MAT/SUB handling costs calculations in (32):

$$\$1.2 \text{ million MAT/SUB handing costs} = \$15 \text{ million} \atop \text{MAT/SUB} \times 8\% \text{ MAT/SUB handing rate} \qquad (32)$$

See Table 11.4 for materials and subcontract costs added to the model.

Table 11.4 Materials and subcontracts

Top-level labor categories	Indirect rate (%)	Labor hours	Labor rate ($/hour)	Total
Design Engineering		13,333	$75.00	$1,000,000
Operations Engineering		7,857	$70.00	$550,000
Production		<u>60,000</u>	$50.00	<u>$3,000,000</u>
Total Direct Labor		**81,190**		**$4,550,000**
Total Fringe	37			$1,683,500
Total Overhead	95			$4,322,500
Materials/Subcontracts				$15,000,000
MAT/SUB Handling	8			$1,200,000

Other Direct Costs, Travel, and Total Nonlabor

Companies typically combine travel and ODC in a budget category
called nonlabor. ODC generally includes miscellaneous direct costs such
as printing and outside consulting. Companies often burden ODC and
travel costs with G&A. The term "burdened" refers to allocating a category of indirect costs to a direct base using a specific indirect rate. Travel
and ODC costs are usually low compared to other expenditures like
direct labor, except possibly for projects with frequent international
travel; therefore, they are rarely significant sources of cost overruns. Assume $50,000 of travel costs and $100,000 of ODC. Total nonlabor
is the sum of materials/subcontracts, MAT/SUB handling, travel, and
ODC costs, but doesn't include fringe and overhead which are calculated based on direct labor. Total nonlabor costs for the example are in
Table 11.5.

Table 11.5 ODC, travel, and total nonlabor

Top-level labor categories	Indirect rate (%)	Labor hours	Labor rate ($/hour)	Total
Design Engineering		13,333	$75.00	$1,000,000
Operations Engineering		7,857	$70.00	$550,000
Production		60,000	$50.00	$3,000,000
Total Direct Labor		81,190		**$4,550,000**
Total Fringe	37			$1,683,500
Total Overhead	95			$4,322,500
Materials/Subcontracts				$15,000,000
MAT/SUB Handling	8			$1,200,000
Travel				$50,000
ODC				$100,000
Total Nonlabor				**$16,350,000**

General and Administrative Costs

The next step is to include the G&A allocation. Because G&A costs
are enterprise-wide, the G&A base must also be enterprise-wide. The
G&A rate equals total G&A costs divided by the G&A base. G&A

typically includes enterprise-wide costs like executive, finance, HR, and IT salaries. The G&A base sums direct labor, fringe, materials handling, subcontract handling (but not materials and subcontracts, which have separate rates), overhead, travel, and ODC costs. Assume the company's G&A rate is 35 percent. See G&A calculations in (33) and (34) and costs in Table 11.6.

$$\$11,906,000 \text{ G\&A base} = \$4,550,000 \text{ direct labor}$$
$$+ \$1,683,500 \text{ fringe} + \$4,332,500 \text{ OH}$$
$$+ \$1,200,000 \text{ MAT/SUB handing} \tag{33}$$
$$+ \$50,000 \text{ travel} + \$100,000 \text{ ODC}$$

$$\$4,167,100 \text{ total G\&A} = \$11,906,000 \text{ G\&A base} \tag{34}$$
$$\times 35\% \text{ G\&A rate}$$

Table 11.6 G&A

Top-level labor categories	Indirect rate (%)	Labor hours	Labor rate ($/hour)	Total
Design Engineering		13,333	$75.00	$1,000,000
Operations Engineering		7,857	$70.00	$550,000
Production		<u>60,000</u>	$50.00	<u>$3,000,000</u>
Total Direct Labor		**81,190**		**$4,550,000**
Total Fringe	37			$1,683,500
Total Overhead	95			$4,322,500
Materials/Subcontracts				$15,000,000
MAT/SUB Handling	8			$1,200,000
Travel				$50,000
<u>ODC</u>				<u>$100,000</u>
Total Nonlabor				**$16,350,000**
G&A Base				$11,906,000
Total G&A	35			$4,167,100

Total Direct, Total Indirect, and All Costs

We can now calculate total direct and indirect costs in (35) to (37):

$$\begin{aligned}
\$19,700,000 \text{ total direct costs} = \$4,550,000 \\
+ \$15 \text{ million MAT/SUB handing} + \$50,000 \text{ travel} \\
+ \$100,000 \text{ ODC}
\end{aligned} \quad (35)$$

$$\begin{aligned}
\$11,373,100 \text{ total indirect costs} = \$1,683,500 \text{ fringe} \\
+ 4,322,500 \text{ OH} + \$1,200,000 \text{ MAT/SUB handing} \\
+ \$4,167,100 \text{ G\&A}
\end{aligned} \quad (36)$$

$$\begin{aligned}
\$31,073,100 \text{ total costs} = \$19,700,000 \text{ total direct costs} \\
+ \$11,373,100 \text{ total indirect costs}
\end{aligned} \quad (37)$$

Table 11.7 adds total direct costs, total indirect costs, and total costs to the model.

Table 11.7 Direct, indirect, and total costs

Top-level labor categories	Indirect rate (%)	Labor hours	Labor rate ($/hour)	Total
Design Engineering		13,333	$75.00	$1,000,000
Operations Engineering		7,857	$70.00	$550,000
Production		60,000	$50.00	$3,000,000
Total Direct Labor		81,190		**$4,550,000**
Total Fringe	37			$1,683,500
Total Overhead	95			$4,322,500
Materials/Subcontracts				$15,000,000
MAT/SUB Handling	8			$1,200,000
Travel				$50,000
ODC				$100,000
Total Nonlabor				**$16,350,000**
G&A Base				$11,906,000
Total G&A	35			$4,167,100
Total Direct Costs				$19,700,000
Total Indirect Costs				$11,373,100
Total Costs				**$31,073,100**

Fee

The fee is the project's profit, calculated as a percentage of the total cost. Assume a target fee of 15 percent. The fee is calculated in (38) and shown in Table 11.8.

$$\$4{,}660{,}965 \text{ fee} = \$31{,}073{,}100 \text{ total cost} \times 15\% \qquad (38)$$

Table 11.8 Fee

Top-level labor categories	Indirect rate (%)	Labor hours	Labor rate ($/hour)	Total
Design Engineering		13,333	$75.00	$1,000,000
Operations Engineering		7,857	$70.00	$550,000
Production		<u>60,000</u>	$50.00	<u>$3,000,000</u>
Total Direct Labor		81,190		**$4,550,000**
Total Fringe	37			$1,683,500
Total Overhead	95			$4,322,500
Materials/Subcontracts				$15,000,000
MAT/SUB Handling	8			$1,200,000
Travel				$50,000
ODC				<u>$100,000</u>
Total Nonlabor				**$16,350,000**
G&A Base				$11,906,000
Total G&A	35			$4,167,100
Total Direct Costs				$19,700,000
Total Indirect Costs				<u>$11,373,100</u>
Total Costs				**$31,073,100**
Fee	15			$4,660,965

Cost of Money and Total Price

Direct labor, materials/subcontracts, and G&A base are pools of money that cost money. The Cost of Money (COM) is indirect, so the company must allocate it to the final price. A company does not add value to the COM because the capital markets and the Federal Reserve determine capital costs. Because a company doesn't add value to the COM, it should calculate the fee as a percentage of total costs *before* adding in the COM.

There may be multiple categories of COM, typically for overhead (COM-OH), materials and subcontracts (COM-MAT/SUB), and G&A (COM-G&A). For our example, assume the COM-OH rate is 1.0 percent, the COM-MAT/SUB rate is 0.8 percent, and the COM-G&A rate is 0.9 percent. See COM-OH calculations in (39), for COM-MAT/SUB in (40), and for COM-G&A in (41). Total COM calculations are in (42). Total price calculations are in (43). The final pricing table is in Table 11.9.

$$\$45,500 \text{ COM} - \text{OH} = 0.01 \times \$4,550,000 \text{ direct labor} \tag{39}$$

$$\$120,000 \text{ COM} - \text{MAT/SUB} = 0.008 \times \$15 \text{ million MAT/SUB} \tag{40}$$

$$\$107,154 \text{ COM} - \text{G\&A} = 0.009 \times \$11,906,000 \text{ G\&A base} \tag{41}$$

$$\$272,654 \text{ total COM} = \$45,500 \text{ COM} - \text{OH} + \$120,000 \text{ COM} - \text{MAT/SUB} + \$107,154 \text{ COM} - \text{G\&A} \tag{42}$$

$$\$36,006,719 \text{ total price} = \$31,073,100 \text{ total cost} + \$4,660,965 \text{ fee} + \$272,654 \text{ total COM} \tag{43}$$

Table 11.9 COM *and total price*

Top-level labor categories	Indirect rate (%)	Labor hours	Labor rate ($/hour)	Total
Design Engineering		13,333	$75.00	$1,000,000
Operations Engineering		7,857	$70.00	$550,000
Production		60,000	$50.00	$3,000,000
Total Direct Labor		**81,190**		**$4,550,000**
Total Fringe	37			$1,683,500
Total Overhead	95			$4,322,500
Materials/Subcontracts				$15,000,000
MAT/SUB Handling	8			$1,200,000
Travel				$50,000
ODC				$100,000
Total Nonlabor				**$16,350,000**
G&A Base				$11,906,000
Total G&A	35			$4,167,100
Total Direct Costs				$19,700,000
Total Indirect Costs				$11,373,100
Total Costs				**$31,073,100**
Fee	15			$4,660,965
COM				
Overhead	1.00			$45,500
Materials/Subcontracts	0.80			$120,000
G&A	0.90			$107,154
Total COM				**$272,654**
Total Price				**$36,006,719**

Conclusions: Calculating Bottom-Up Estimates for Pricing Decisions

Although the bottom-up calculations appear detailed and thorough, the estimates are likely overly optimistic. Other pricing techniques, such as value, dynamic, premium, psychological, and market pricing, can act as reality checks. RCF is also highly effective in providing a reality check. While the other pricing techniques are beyond the scope of this book, using even one of them can reveal unjustified optimism.

Many companies, especially government contractors, estimate pricing for bids and proposals primarily using bottom-up estimating. They rarely employ RCF because most companies don't require that estimators use it. While these companies may use other pricing techniques described earlier to enhance their pricing strategies, those methods are designed for pricing purposes rather than cost estimating.

This discussion may feel pessimistic. While it's great that people are generally optimistic, this can be a disadvantage when making schedules and cost estimates. If you take the conventional route and accept the cost estimates on their own merits, at least consider what you'll do if you lose the bet and overruns occur. Most individuals who approve forecasts are not involved in executing the project. Consequently, if the project overruns, they often blame the project team for poor execution. Their first action should be reexamining their original assumptions and expectations to determine if their approved estimates were realistic. Most of the time, they'll find the original projections were highly unrealistic.

A line of business that reported to me bid on a follow-up order for a complex satellite antenna pointing mechanism. Only a handful of units were built and flown. Since the previous project team completed their contract, the new project team relied on historical data from the prior project to develop their schedule and cost estimates. But there was a problem.

The previous project team had extensive, *undocumented* knowledge and expertise of how to build the product, but all of them had since left the company. When the new project team developed their schedule and cost estimates, they didn't account for the time required to relearn how to build the product. As a result, the project overran. Be careful: challenge your assumptions!

Summary

Product pricing is either determined top-down, based on market forces, or bottom-up, by rolling up cost estimates and then adding profit to arrive at a target price. It's also common to adjust the bottom-up price to account for market dynamics. Either way, at some point, you must take your costs into account when developing a price to ensure you will make money. If blind spots cause your estimates to be optimistic, the product may sell well, but you'll lose money. Most cost estimates include a detailed examination of the work scope, labor hours, and materials required to do the job. Many estimators add some padding to account for uncertainty and estimation errors.

However, they still tend to substantially underestimate cost increases due to learning, multitasking, random variation, and especially external influences like unplanned scope changes, equipment or design failures, and many others. The only way to account for unplanned cost increases is to look at what others have done of a similar size and complexity. If their costs were $10 million, and you estimate $4 million for yours, *what are you missing*? It's unlikely the other party's team is completely incompetent, and it's equally unlikely that your team is far more competent to justify a 60 percent lower cost. If you can't explain the discrepancy, then at least include a cost reserve.

If you're responsible for managing costs, learn financial definitions such as direct and indirect costs, contribution margins, indirect rates, and BOEs. As mentioned above, cost estimators tend to underestimate costs because they fail to account for all the variables. However, another blind spot is not understanding how their indirect rate model impacts their business model. They also typically don't know how contribution margins can help fund sales growth and absorb spare manufacturing capacity.

If you work for a government contractor or any contract-driven business, you'll likely be developing bottom-up cost and schedule estimates for bids and proposals. This chapter can help you make your proposals more realistic and achievable.

As customer needs and market conditions change, products and services must adapt to them, implying that product development is an ongoing cycle. Hopefully, you'll find this book helpful throughout every stage of product development, across multiple product development cycles and projects.

Reader Call to Action

Build up a cost model for your product or service. No matter how conservative you try to be, your estimates will likely be highly optimistic unless you use actual costs from past, similar projects.

1. How will you ensure your cost estimates are accurate?
2. Are you budgeting for any reserves in the estimates?
   a. What's your rationale for how much to reserve?
3. Are the indirect rates correct and officially approved?
   a. Are any indirect rate changes pending? A rate increase drives an immediate cost increase to the project. Do you have reserves to cover this?
4. Are the labor hour estimates correct?
   a. Labor hours are often highly optimistic because of unplanned mistakes, requirements changes, optimism, and the failure to use RCF to challenge assumptions.
5. Are materials and subcontract costs correct, and do they include reserves?
   a. The more competitive the procurement process, the more likely vendors' delivery schedules will be optimistic, which leads to delays that drive overruns.
6. Did you compare your final cost estimate against outside actuals from RCF?

Lessons Learned

1. Cost estimators build up costs incrementally, starting with direct labor hours, converting direct labor hours to dollars, adding in materials costs and ODC (travel, consulting), and then burdening the direct costs with indirect costs and fee. Direct costs like labor and materials vary directly with production volume and can be charged directly to a product, project, or contract. However, indirect costs like office space, lighting, or equipment are constant, so companies must allocate them to product unit prices.

2. Labor hour forecasts estimate how long it will take to complete tasks. They're typically wildly optimistic. However, additional errors exist because companies normally average labor rates used in cost estimates across junior and senior labor categories. Estimators average the labor rates because the resources that will work on a future task are often unknown.

3. If both labor hour and labor rate estimates are optimistic, their errors combine to produce optimistic labor cost estimates. Regardless of how detailed or justified a bottom-up cost estimate appears, it will likely be optimistic, especially if management reduces it to achieve a competitive price-to-win target.

4. A company's indirect rate structure can significantly impact its competitive position and pricing. High indirect cost allocations can make a product's price uncompetitive.

5. If a product isn't selling well and a company has spare capacity, an effective short-term strategy is to reduce the unit price to a level higher than direct costs but less than total costs. The difference between the price and direct costs *contributes* to partially covering (absorbing) indirect costs that otherwise wouldn't be covered. To survive over the long term, a company must charge a high enough price to cover *all* costs plus a reasonable profit.

6. The best way to surface hidden, unjustified optimism in your cost estimates is to leverage RCF. Challenge your assumptions by learning from history.

Conclusion

Now that you've invested the time and energy into reading this book, you know how to ensure your new product helps customers achieve their most important desired results. You're also serious about preventing schedule and cost overruns.

If you learn only one thing from this book, it should be to watch for blind spots in all stages of new product development that arise from unjustified optimism. Do you know what your customers want? If you think you do, how can you be sure? *What evidence supports your beliefs?* Are your development project's schedule and budget targets realistic? Do they consider potential causes of delays beyond the usual technical and supplier risks? How will you respond if your assumptions and beliefs prove to be incorrect? It's better to ask these questions upfront and adjust your plans accordingly than to assume everything will work out and you'll deal with future product failures and overruns if and when they occur.

Here's a recap of one key takeaway from each chapter:

1. A customer need is a desired result, not a vague want, product feature, or capability. The best sales opportunities arise when your product significantly increases customers' satisfaction with their most important desired results. Everything else follows from there.

2. Your product represents a value proposition, providing a solution that enables customers to achieve their most important desired results. It's the intersection of a product, a customer, and an application. Altering any one of these elements changes the value proposition. Be sure to include services and support in the value proposition so that customers can use the product successfully.

3. Test and validate your value proposition to deliver the results customers desire. Accomplish this with a written target customer scenario and positioning statement. Don't skip this step, as many companies do!

4. Selling to key stakeholders follows the same approach as selling to external customers. Do you know what your stakeholders'

important desired results are? Does your solution deliver those desired results more effectively than current solutions? Are you providing a foundation of truth rather than subjective opinions?

5. Unless your project is simple, use a project management system, such as critical path, EV, critical chain, or agile, along with commercial project management software. Monitor the progress of key activities that serve as leading indicators for schedule and cost overruns.

6. Most companies believe that poor supplier performance and technical issues are the primary causes of overruns. While these are significant factors, a key blind spot is that many other underlying habits often go unnoticed. Collectively, these behaviors contribute to unrealistic and unjustified optimism in baseline plans, which leads to overruns:

   a. Failing to recognize and manage uncertainty.
   b. Using aggressive targets to avoid overruns.
   c. Tracking projects using only lagging indicators.
   d. Failing to manage resource overloads.
   e. Funding projects without reserves to protect against overruns.
   f. Underestimating due to the planning fallacy.
   g. Adopting a get-it-sold-and-keep-it-sold mindset.
   h. Assessing risks optimistically.
   i. Underinvesting in technical execution.
   j. Exhibiting unjustified optimism.

7. Most companies measure progress against their strategic goals. However, they often fail to track the progress of key activities that drive those results. To stay ahead of the project, identify, measure, and track the leading activities that drive each strategic goal.

8. Let history guide you when estimating schedules and costs. What have you or others done that is similar in size and complexity? If your estimates are more aggressive than historical data, what sets your team apart?

9. Manage resource capacity to prevent overruns. Maintain resource utilization between 50 and 60 percent, especially in groups supporting product development projects, as resource productivity decreases significantly and user wait times for service increase dramatically beyond this threshold.

10. Avoid using mathematical expected values to forecast sales unless you have enough statistical data to back up your probability estimates. Instead, rely on sales funnel dropout rates to predict sales and identify the key activities needed to generate those sales, such as leads, sales calls, or conversions.

11. Watch out for blind spots in how you estimate and forecast direct costs, indirect costs, pricing, sales volume, and revenue. The same forces that cause unjustified optimism in market, schedule, and cost estimates also affect budget estimates and pricing.

Incentives are a big blind spot that causes product failures and overruns. Companies design their systems to drive performance and growth. As a result, people feel intense pressure to perform to ensure job security. If competitive pressures cause management to impose aggressive performance targets, individuals have limited incentives to plan and forecast conservatively. These pressures escalate as competition increases. The outcome is overly optimistic forecasts and commitments.

You should take action to identify and address blind spots that often lead to unjustified optimism in market, schedule, and cost targets, and forecasts and pricing estimates. You probably can't change most human habits or incentives. However, you can ask how estimates compare to past performance internally or elsewhere; establish schedule and budget reserves; limit resource utilization to less than 60 percent by controlling the flow of work through bottlenecks; measure resistance to project workflow; and identify and track leading activities that drive progress toward achieving strategic goals like schedule and cost performance.

As the saying goes, "Nothing destroys a good argument like data."[33] You can use the techniques in this book to gather data that will help you develop a foundation of truth to support arguments for change.

If this book helps you become more successful, please let me know. I'd be delighted to hear about it!

---

[33] *Karl Popper*, a philosopher of science known for his work on the philosophy of science and falsifying data. I didn't find definitive evidence of Popper directly using this phrase in his writings, so it may be a paraphrase or a misattribution.

Glossary

Actual Value (AV): Also called the Actual Cost of Work Performed (ACWP), refers to the actual costs incurred at a specific point in time. Used to evaluate project performance.

Agile Development: An iterative development approach, primarily for software, that emphasizes flexibility, collaboration, customer satisfaction, and continuous improvement. It emphasizes delivering working software in iterative, small increments, allowing for frequent feedback and updates throughout the development life cycle.

Allocation: A proration of a budget pool over a relevant base, such as total overhead costs divided by total direct labor dollars.

Artificial Intelligence (AI): The use of computer systems to perform tasks that typically require human intelligence, such as learning and decision-making.

Augmented Product: Adds value to the Generic and Expected Products by providing customers with additional services that replace tasks they currently handle, saving them time and money. See the Whole Product.

Baseline: An approved plan that provides a reference for measuring project performance.

Basis of Estimate (BOE): Documentation detailing how a cost estimate was developed, including assumptions and data sources.

Benchmarking: The process of comparing a company's processes or performance against industry leaders to identify areas for improvement.

Blind Spots: In the context of this book, blind spots refer to policies, practices, procedures, or behaviors in new product development and project management that practitioners are often unaware of, but that frequently lead to product-market failures and cost and schedule overruns.

Bottom-Up Cost Estimates: An estimating method that aggregates costs from individual tasks up through the entire project level, to form a complete project budget or contract price.

Buffer Ratio: A metric comparing the length of the project buffer to the remaining duration along a project's critical path. Used to assess schedule risk.

Contribution Margin (CM): Revenue minus variable costs. The difference absorbs fixed costs.

Cost of Money (COM): The opportunity cost of using capital. It's the COM tied up in inventory and indirect cost pools.

Cost Performance Index (CPI): The ratio of earned value to actual costs. Measures a project's cost efficiency by relating work completed to actual costs.

Critical Chain: The critical path (see critical path) with a project buffer (see project buffer) added to protect against schedule slips due to uncertainties and unplanned resource conflicts.

Critical Chain Project Management (CCPM): A method that emphasizes resource constraints and buffer management to ensure on-time delivery.

Critical Path: The longest sequence of project activities through a project's task network. Determines the project's minimum duration.

Critical Path Project Management (CPPM): A scheduling technique that identifies the sequence of tasks, known as the critical path, that determines the project duration.

Cycle Time: The total elapsed time it takes for one unit of work to move through a single process step or the entire process, from start to finish.

Direct Costs: Expenses directly associated with a specific project, contract, product, or service, such as raw materials or direct labor.

Direct Labor: The portion of labor costs directly traceable to executing a specific project, contract, product, or service.

Earned Value (EV): Also called the Budgeted Cost of Work Performmed (BCWP). Represents the value of planned work that is complete.

Earned Value Management System (EVMS): A project management framework that integrates scope, schedule, and cost to assess performance and forecast outcomes.

Estimate at Complete (EAC): A forecast of the total expected project cost based on performance to date.

Estimate to Complete (ETC): An estimate of the costs required to finish the remaining planned and unplanned project work.

Expected Product: Adds Technical support, Quality, Responsiveness, Delivery, and Cost (TQRDC) to the Generic Product layer of the Whole Product (see the Whole Product). Services and support are necessary for customers to use products effectively.

Expected Value: A probabilistic estimate representing the weighted average of all possible outcomes.

Fixed Costs: Costs that remain constant regardless of production volume, like rent or salaries.

Fringe Costs: Indirect compensation expenses for benefits like health insurance, vacation pay, and corporate retirement contributions.

Full Time Equivalent (FTE): One person working 40 hours per week for 49 weeks per year, including three weeks of vacation.

G&A Base: Total enterprise cost. Used as the base for calculating the general and administrative (G&A) indirect rate.

G&A Costs: Enterprise-wide expenses for business management not tied to a specific project, such as accounting or HR.

G&A Rate: The percentage rate used to allocate G&A costs across the G&A base (see G&A base).

Generic Product: The core product or service customers buy, without additional layers of the Whole Product (see the Whole Product). The innermost layer of the Whole Product.

Ideal Customer Profile: A detailed description of the type of customer who would benefit most from and be most likely to buy a product or service.

Indirect Costs: Expenses not directly associated with a specific project, contract, product, or service, such as utilities or administrative support.

Indirect Rates: The percentages used to allocate indirect costs, such as overhead or fringe, to specific cost objectives like direct labor or direct materials. Used to allocate indirect costs to direct costs in pricing calculations.

Just-in-Time (JIT): A manufacturing and process management strategy that pulls materials at each process step according to the using step's demand, instead of a traditional push system that relies on forecasts and builds inventory. A demand-pull system minimizes waste, materials management costs, and inefficiencies by synchronizing supply with demand.

Lagging Metric: A performance indicator that measures past outcomes, often strategic and financial goals such as market share, revenue, or profit. Because the outcomes are in the past, the metric always lags what it measures.

Lead Time: The amount of time between the initiation of a process and its completion, such as the time from order placement to delivery.

Leading Metric: A predictive indicator that measures the performance of key activities that drive progress toward strategic goals. Because leading activities precede strategic outcomes, leading metrics provide early signals of future strategic outcomes.

Materials and Subcontracts (MATSUB) Costs: Direct costs for physical goods and third-party services required to complete a project.

Materials Handling (MH) Costs: Indirect costs for moving, storing, and managing materials used in production or projects.

Materials Handling Rate: The percentage applied to direct material costs to calculate materials handling expenses, to allocate them over the direct materials base.

Multitasking: Simultaneously performing multiple tasks instead of sequencing them. Often reduces overall productivity due to task-switching inefficiencies.

Nonlabor Costs: Expenses unrelated to people, such as materials, equipment, travel, or software used in a project.

Original Equipment Manufacturer (OEM): A company that produces parts or equipment that may be marketed by another company under its own brand.

Other Direct Costs (ODC): Direct project costs not categorized as labor or materials, such as travel and printing costs.

Overhead Costs: Indirect business expenses that support production. Examples include production facilities, capital equipment depreciation, and lighting.

Overhead Rate: A percentage used to allocate overhead expenses across a direct cost base, typically direct labor.

Overrun: The amount by which actual project costs or durations exceed planned or budgeted amounts, in absolute or percentage terms.

Planned Value (PV): Also called the Budgeted Cost of Work Scheduled (BCWS), refers to the planned cost of work that the project should have completed through the end of the current reporting period.

Positioning Statement: A concise, two-sentence statement of a product's unique value, target customer, and competitive differentiation.

Potential Product: The outermost layer of the Whole Product. Leverages new opportunities driven by changes in customers' environments, cost structures, or their customers' environments to add value.

Process Speed: The rate at which a process completes its intended task.

Project Buffer: A time-only, non-resourced task added to the end of a project's critical path (see critical path). It absorbs delays and protects the project's final completion date.

Project Management Review (PMR): A recurring, usually monthly, meeting between key stakeholders like project teams, management, and sometimes customers to review a project's progress, issues, spending, and risks.

Project Scope: Identifies the work required to complete a project. Includes deliverables and defines the boundaries between what the project will and will not accomplish.

Queuing Theory: A branch of mathematics that models the behavior of queues or waiting lines. Used to study systems like resource servers, where users must wait while the servers are busy working on other projects.

Reference Class Forecasting (RCF): A forecasting method that uses knowledge of other, similar projects to adjust schedule or cost estimates for bias.

Request for Proposal (RFP): A formal document issued to solicit bids from vendors for goods or services.

Reserves: Funds or resources set aside in a project budget as insurance against unknown risks like unplanned scope and requirements changes.

Resistance Metric (RM): The percentage of the passage of time in a reporting period during which the project did not complete any work. Measures the resistance against a project's workflow because of bureaucracy, mistakes, and other possible causes.

Resource Buffer: Time-only, non-resourced tasks added to the end of each slack path in a project's task network (see slack path). A resource buffer absorbs delays to prevent a slack path from slipping so much that it causes the project's critical path to slip.

Risk Management: The process of identifying, analyzing, and mitigating risks that may affect project outcomes.

Risk Register: A list of risks, probability of occurrence, value, and associated mitigation plans.

Sales Funnel: A conceptual model describing the customer journey from awareness to purchase. The model uses a funnel metaphor because customers drop out at each stage of the process.

Sales Opportunities Quad Chart: A visual tool to identify sales opportunities. Plots customer needs as a function of their perceived importance and satisfaction.

Schedule Performance Index (SPI): The ratio of earned value (see earned value) to planned value (see planned value). Measures a project's schedule efficiency.

Stakeholder: Anyone with an interest in or influence on the success of a project.

Target Customer Scenario: A hypothetical narrative that describes customers' experiences before and after a new product or service is available, to test whether a product or service successfully meets customers' needs.

Task Network: A diagram that maps the sequence and dependencies of tasks within a project. Used to calculate the project's critical path (see critical path), baseline schedule (see baseline), and to track a project's schedule performance.

The Planning Fallacy: A human cognitive bias where people underestimate the time and resources required to complete future tasks. Results from a natural tendency to overlook past experiences or potential risks.

Throughput: The rate at which a system produces outputs. Often used as a productivity metric.

TQRDC: A memory mnemonic for Technical support, Quality, Responsiveness, Delivery, and Cost. It refers to the Expected Product (see Expected Product), which is the services and support layer of the Whole Product (see Whole Product). Ensures that customers can use a product or service effectively.

Unfavorable Variance: The amount in absolute or percentage terms where actual performance is worse than planned, such as higher costs or delayed tasks.

Unjustified Optimism: Overconfidence in future, positive outcomes without sufficient data or risk assessment to justify the estimate.

Value Proposition: The intersection of a product or service, the customer type, and the application. If any of these variables change, the value proposition will also change.

Value-Added Work Content: Work that directly contributes to transforming a product or service to fulfill customer requirements or improve the product's value.

Variable Costs: Costs that fluctuate in proportion to the production or sales rate. Variable costs are usually, but not always, direct costs.

Variance: The absolute or percentage difference between planned and actual outcomes in budget, time, or scope. Used as a performance metric. A variance may be favorable, where actual performance is better than planned, or unfavorable, where actual performance is worse than planned.

Whole Product: The complete customer value proposition, including all layers (see Generic Product, Expected Product, Augmented Product, and Potential Product).

Work Breakdown Structure (WBS): A hierarchical outline that decomposes project scope into manageable components and deliverables.

Workload Metric: A measure of the quantity of work assigned or completed by a resource or group of resources, as a percentage of average project length. Used to sequence work to avoid resource overloads or underloads and optimize throughput.

Resources

Templates and workbooks to help you apply the book's analysis techniques and metrics to your data are available for download on the author's website at www.targemetrics.com/resources. They also include example content.

- Bottom-Up Pricing Analysis Worksheet
- Cumulative Line Chart Worksheet
- Desired Results and Sales Opportunities Quad Chart Analysis Workbook
- PMR Quad Chart Template
- Positioning Statement Template
- Resistance Metric Worksheet
- Risk Analysis Worksheet
- Sales Funnel Dropout Worksheet
- Target Customer Scenario Template
- Value Proposition Template
- Whole Product Model Workbook
- Workload Metric Analysis Worksheet

References

Some government websites are blocked for international access. Contact the author at info@targemetrics.com for a copy of the source.

Balka, Kerstin, Breanna Heslin, and Sina Risse-Tenk. "Unlocking the Potential of Public-Sector IT Projects." *McKinsey.com.* 2022. Accessed June 23, 2025. https://www.mckinsey.com/industries/public-sector/our-insights/unlocking-the-potential-of-public-sector-it-projects.

Bradley, Chris, Martin Hirt, and Sven Smit. "Have You Tested Your Strategy Lately?" *McKinsey Quarterly.* 2011. Accessed June 23, 2025. https://www.mckinsey.com/capabilities/strategy-and-corporate-finance/our-insights/have-you-tested-your-strategy-lately.

Clark, Stephen. "Boeing's Starliner Has Cost at Least Twice as Much as SpaceX's Crew Dragon." *Ars Technica.* 2024. Accessed June 23, 2025. https://arstechnica.com/space/2024/07/boeing-warns-of-more-financial-losses-on-starliner-commercial-crew-program/.

Defense Acquisition University. "Earned Value Management General Reference (Gold Card)." 2024. Accessed June 23, 2025. https://www.dau.edu/tools/earned-value-management-general-reference-gold-card.

DeMuro, Jonas P. "Best Project Management Software." *Techradar.* 2025. Accessed June 23, 2025. https://www.techradar.com/best/best-project-management-software.

Flyvbjerg, Bent, and Alexander Budzier. "Why Your IT Project May Be Riskier Than You Think." *Harvard Business Review.* 2011. Accessed June 23, 2025. https://hbr.org/2011/09/why-your-it-project-may-be-riskier-than-you-think.

Foust, Jeff (SpaceRef). "NOAA-N-Prime Satellite Mishap Investigation Report Released." *SpaceNews.* 2004. Accessed June 23, 2025. https://spacenews.com/noaa-n-prime-satellite-mishap-investigation-report-released/.

Gartner. "Project Portfolio Management, Worldwide Reviews and Ratings." 2025. Accessed June 23, 2025. https://www.gartner.com/reviews/market/project-portfolio-management-worldwide.

Georgescu, Alexander. "Queueing Theory and Practice." Computer Science Blog @ HdM *Stuttgart.* 2019. Accessed June 23, 2025. https://blog.mi.hdm-stuttgart.de/index.php/2019/03/11/queueing-theory-and-practice-or-crash-course-in-queueing/.

Goldratt, Eliyahu M. *Critical Chain.* The North River Press, 1997.

History.com Editors. "New Coke Debuts, One of the Biggest Product Flops in History." *History.com.* 2025. Accessed June 23, 2025. https://www.history.com/this-day-in-history/new-coke-debuts-one-of-the-biggest-product-flops-in-history.

Holt, James R., and Robin Clark. "Finding the Sweet Spot in Resource Work-load." *ISE Magazine* 50, no. 4 (2018): 32–36. Accessed June 23, 2025. https://extendsim.com/images/downloads/papers/general-ise201804.pdf.

Kahneman, Daniel, and Amos Tversky. "Intuitive Prediction: Biases and Corrective Procedures." *Defense Technical Information Center.* 1977. Accessed June 23, 2025. https://apps.dtic.mil/sti/tr/pdf/ADA047747.pdf.

Kaplan, Robert S., and Steven R. Anderson. "Time-Driven Activity-Based Cost-ing." *Harvard Business Review* 82, no. 11 (2004.): 131–38. Accessed June 23, 2025. https://hbr.org/2004/11/time-driven-activity-based-costing.

Katz, Gerry. "A Critique of Outcome-Driven Innovation." *Applied Marketing Science.* 2008. https://ams-insights.com/article/critique-outcome-driven-innovation/.

Levitt, Theodore. *The Marketing Imagination.* Simon & Schuster, 1983.

McChesney, Chris, Sean Covey, and Jim Huling. *The 4 Disciplines of Execution: Achieving Your Wildly Important Goals.* Free Press, 2012.

McKenna, Regis. *The Regis Touch.* Addison-Wesley, 1985.

Microsoft. "Create a Project in Project Desktop." *Microsoft Support.* n.d. Accessed June 23, 2025. https://support.microsoft.com/en-us/office/create-a-project-in -project-desktop-783c8570-0111-4142-af80-989aabfe29af.

Miller, Robert B., and Stephen E. Heiman, with Tad Tuleja. *Strategic Selling.* William Morrow, 1985.

Moore, Geoffrey A. *Crossing the Chasm.* Harper Business, 1991.

Rotich, Rachel. "Risk Analysis in Project Management: Steps and Bene-fits." *Indeed.com.* 2022. Accessed June 23, 2025. https://www.indeed.com /career-advice/career-development/risk-analysis-project-management.

Rutkowski, Ireneusz. "Success and Failure Rates of New Food and Non-Food Products Introduced on the Market." *Journal of Marketing and Consumer Behaviour in Emerging Markets 1, no. 14 (2022):* 52–61. https://www .researchgate.net/publication/359923834_Success_and_failure_rates_of _new_food_and_non-food_products_introduced_on_the_market.

Schonberger, Richard J. *World Class Manufacturing Casebook: Implementing JIT and TQC.* Macmillan, 1987.

Smith, Marcia. "Boeing's Starliner Losses Reach $2 Billion." *SpacePolicyOnline.com.* 2025. Accessed August 13, 2025. https://spacepolicyonline.com/news /boeings-starliner-losses-reach-2-billion/.

Ulwick, Anthony W. *What Customers Want: Using Outcome-Driven Innovation to Create Breakthrough Products and Services.* McGraw-Hill, 2005.

U.S. Department of Labor. *A Guide for Indirect Cost Rate Determination.* Cost & Price Determination Division, Office of Strategy & Administration/OSPE /OASAM, 2024. https://www.dol.gov/sites/dolgov/files/OASAM/legacy/files /DCD-2-CFR-Guide.pdf.

U.S. GAO (Government Accountability Office). *Cost Estimating and Assessment Guide: Best Practices for Developing and Managing Program Costs.* GAO-20-195G. 2020. https://www.gao.gov/assets/gao-20-195g.pdf.

About the Author

Paul Streit has garnered deep and broad expertise in managing new product development. His work has focused on four major high-tech industries, with experience in organizations ranging from startups to billion-dollar corporations. He has led organizations ranging from startups to over 1,000 employees, guiding leaders in developing custom, one-of-a-kind solutions and mass-produced, high-volume products.

Paul reveals to clients the hidden causes of new product market failures and overruns and how to prevent them from hindering product development efforts, ensuring they can successfully develop products right the first time. He holds a bachelor's degree in biomedical and electronics engineering from Duke University and a master's in business administration from the University of Miami.

When he is not helping clients, Paul travels the world, visits family, reads, skis, sails, and occasionally relearns how to do takeoffs and landings with a longtime flying buddy. He and his wife live in Denver, Colorado, with their adorable dog, who rules the house.

For more information about Paul and his book *Blind Spots: Why Product Development Projects Miss Their Targets*, visit www.targemetrics .com or e-mail info@targemetrics.com.

Thank You for Reading

Blind Spots: Why Product Development Projects Miss Their Targets

If you enjoyed this book, please consider posting a review with honest impressions on Amazon, Goodreads, or another platform. Your feedback is invaluable for improving the book and expanding its reach to a broader audience.

Visit www.targemetrics.com to connect with Paul Streit or book him for consulting, training, or keynote speeches/presentations on preventing new product market failures and overruns.

You can download free analytical resources from Paul's website that you can apply to your own data, and learn about Targemetrics, a discipline Paul developed over decades that provides analytical techniques and innovative metrics to help prevent market failures and overruns.

Or scan the QR code.

Or e-mail at info@targemetrics.com

Index